IRELAND

A Travellers' Guide

IRELAND

A Traveller's
Guide

MARESE MURPHY

HIPPOCRENE
BOOKS, INC.

Distribution:
Distributed in Great Britain and the Commonwealth by
Roger Lascelles, 47 York Road, Brentford, Middlesex TW8 0QP
Telephone: 01-847-0935

ISBN 0 902726 41 2

Distributed in the United States and Canada by
Hippocrene Books Inc., 171 Madison Avenue, New York, NY 10016

US ISBN 0 87052 719 3

Published by Thornton Cox (1986) Ltd,
Epworth House, 23-35 City Road, London EC1Y 1AA

Published in the United States and Canada by
Hippocrene Books Inc., 171 Madison
Avenue, New York, NY 10016

First published 1977. Second edition, 1981. Third edition, 1989

Drawings by Guy Magnus
Maps by Tom Stalker-Miller, MSIA
Series Editor: Kit Harding

Cover:
Dungaire Castle, Co. Galway. This and inside colour photographs
by courtesy of the Irish Tourist Board

*Great care has been taken throughout this book to be accurate, but
the publishers cannot accept responsibility for any errors which appear*

Printed in Great Britain by The Guernsey Press Company Limited,
Guernsey, Channel Islands. Set in 8½ on 9½ pt Univers

© Thornton Cox (1986) Ltd, 1989

Thornton Cox Guides:

Titles in print in this series include:

Kenya	**Greece**
Egypt	**Majorca**
Southern France	**Portugal**

Customs House, Dublin

Contents

Author's Acknowledgements

The author wishes to express sincere appreciation of the generous assistance provided by both the Irish Tourist Board and the Northern Ireland Tourist Board during the research for this book. Special thanks are due to Tim Magennis and Eilis Colbert of the Irish Tourist Board in Dublin, and to Clare McGinn of the Northern Ireland Tourist Board; to Liam O'Hanion, Bobby Johnson, Denis O'Neill and Mary Mcgreal of local tourist offices at Killarney, Sligo, Letterkenny and Westport, and to Colman Garrihy of SFADCO whose enthusiasm, kindness and hospitality make Clare and the Limerick Shannonside the most welcoming regions in Ireland.

The Author

Marèse Murphy was born in Ireland, in Enniscorthy, Co. Wexford, in 1931. She grew up in Dublin and was educated at Dominican College, Eccles Street, and at University College Dublin. In 1967 she moved to Britain and has lived there since, dividing her time between London and Dorset and working as a freelance writer specialising in arts topics, books and travel. Her principal interests are music, literature, art, history, travel and cookery.

Foreword

To write about Ireland is to challenge a nation of caustic commentators; to be Irish and write about Ireland is to take one's good name in one's hands and risk losing old friendships for ever.

I was born in Ireland, grew up and lived there for nearly forty years: long enough to form a fine volume of prejudices of my own, to accept others ready-made, and to reject quite a number that seemed outlandish, to me at least. This said, what follows is an account of one of the loveliest countries in the world, a country where progress has not yet made too much difference to old customs and manners, still less to the marvellous landscape; a country where intense national chauvinism makes eager friends for anyone who likes the place — which, by the rules governing travel abroad, few can fail to do.

To those who know the country, however, the changes which have taken place over the pasty fifty years seem dramatic; and they are generally, though not always, for the better.

The most important is the spectacular improvement in the standard of living. Thirty years ago Ireland was a backward place, well behind the rest of Europe, with a shoddy daily life, and often a menial cast of mind to go with it. The leap to relative affluence has been accomplished with remarkable speed, and only the most diehard and selfish of conservatives would begrudge the small cost represented by the inevitable sacrifice of some traditional quaintnesses: poverty can be picturesque in the eye of the beholder, but the sentimentalists who bewail the passing of the open fire or the coming of piped water are rarely the people who have to get down on their knees to clean out the former or drag heavy buckets from the well every day. All the same, the rash of "hacienda" - style development disfiguring the west of the country remains one of the more deplorable aspects of progress. It is as if the entire population of the region went on holiday to Spain and returned determined to enshrine the more blatant characteristics of alien architecture in a landscape wholly at odds with it.

Today Ireland is reckoned amongst the developed countries of Europe, active in the EEC and the UN and, despite economic problems of breathtaking proportions, savouring a degree of prosperity in approximate line with the rest of the Western world. There are attendant problems of course. Rapid advances tend to produce paradoxical side-effects, and these can result in piquant contrasts of mind and matter, as marked in social attitudes as they are in the fervent embrace of the hacienda.

One happy outcome of Ireland's sad past is the amazing wealth of

Foreword

historic monuments that have survived in almost every area. Because of its history the country was not in a position to sweep away the landmarks of former times in the manner of so many other nations which developed earlier. In this present period of enlightenment, when historic remains are at last being rightly prized, the Irish therefore have more than their share of treasures, and are showing appreciation of this heritage in fervent programmes of conservation and restoration — except in Dublin, where the City Fathers have given their blessing to desecration of wanton dimensions.

The visitor will find the scenery of Ireland superb; and the people, whose temperament seems to have more to do with the Mediterranean than with the Atlantic, endlessly hospitable and friendly. They have a real sympathy for the problems of others, and also a philosophical and useful habit of accepting life as it comes: if it rains today, it will surely be fine tomorrow, or if not then, the day after. . . . And whatever else, there is always the fishing and the hunting and the shooting, the vast beaches and the swimming and the sailing, the golf, the walking, the climbing — almost every outdoor sport, in fact, that does not depend on extremes of climate for its exercise.

If all this fails to appeal, and if the rain does not stop for a week, there are still the pubs and the parties and an easy-going social life in which visitors become as rapidly and enjoyably immersed as people who have lived in Ireland all their lives. Above all, there is the inimitable Irish gift for the absurd. This verges frequently on surrealism, and is the source of hilarious and off-beat incidents which simply could not occur anywhere else. No outsider can be expected to believe the stories about Ireland — until at last the sceptic joins the millions of travellers who have gone there in their time and become involved in events that could not happen but, somehow, did.

General Information

How to get there

By Air

Ireland's national airline, Aer Lingus, operates regular and frequent services from most European capitals, and, in pool with British Airways, about a dozen cities in Britain have connections with Dublin, Belfast, Shannon, Cork and the new Horan Airport in the West. Some routes are operated by smaller companies, and the young independent Irish airline, Ryanair, has been instrumental in developing traffic direct from Britain to Waterford and Galway. This company has also pioneered the campaign to rationalise fare structures between Britain and Ireland. These vary tremendously in accordance with booking conditions and it is worth consulting a travel agent before parting with your money. Ryanair and Virgin Airlines are in the vanguard for value, with the former also offering first-class fly-drive holidays that are considered highly satisfactory. In 1988 the cheapest return air fare between Dublin and London was £57.00.

The principal Continental airlines are represented in Dublin, and there are also regular flights to the major American cities. Transatlantic flights land at Dublin and Shannon, with passengers changing aircraft to go on to the North, or else landing at Heathrow and changing there for flights to Belfast. Charters and advance-purchase excursion flights bought months before departure effect a considerable saving in the transatlantic fare, though by far the cheapest way to have a holiday in Ireland remains the package tour, comprising flight, accommodation and coach tour or self-drive car.

By Sea

There are seven sea routes from Britain to Ireland, and two from the Continent. All of them are drive-on/drive-off car ferries operated, depending on the port in question, by British Rail's 'Sealink' service, P & O European Ferries, B + I Line, Swansea-Cork Car Ferries, Belfast Car Ferries, Irish Continental Line and Brittany Ferries. Ports of embarkation from Britain include Fishguard, Holyhead, Liverpool, Swansea, Stranraer and Cairnryan. Continental boat services operate from Le Havre to Cork and Rosslare, from Cherbourg to Rosslare, and from Roscoff to Cork.

General Information

On sailings from Britain the B + I boats have the edge over their competitors for comfort and aimiable service, and their restaurant has a reasonable buffet which usually includes a classic joint of beef, lamb or pork.

In 1988 the single fare for a car and driver with four passengers travelling from Holyhead to Dun Laoghaire was £59.50, though again there are seasonal concession rates and special short-stay fares.

For those with the stamina to face a coach journey just short of twelve hours in duration, the best value of all is the £29.00 return bus fare from Dublin to Paddington in London and back again.

Travel within the Country

Air
Internal flights in Ireland now include services between Dublin and Sligo, Dublin and Waterford, and Dublin and Donegal. There are regular flights from the West to the Aran Islands, while those travelling between Northern Ireland and the Republic have the choice of air services between Londonderry and Dublin, and between Belfast and Dublin. The larger airports provide bus services to the relevant city centres, but there is a degree of hit-and-miss about public transport at the smaller places.

Rail and Bus
There are train services between all the major towns and cities in Ireland, and long-distance bus services as well. The two-and-a-half hour train journey from Dublin to Cork costs IR£27.50; IR£17.00 by bus. Special 'Rambler' and 'Overlander' tickets enable visitors to travel about the country at will, and both CIE in the Republic and Ulsterbus in Northern Ireland operate inclusive tours.

Road
Technically, traffic keeps to the left in Ireland, though because of inadequate cambering, there is a tendency to drive in the **middle** of minor roads. The trunk routes from Dublin to Cork, Galway, Belfast and Limerick are good, while lesser roads outside the towns and cities are remarkably free of traffic. As the natives know this, too, it is prudent to remain alert for tractors surging suddenly out of concealed gateways, accelerating as they come in the happy assumption that the road is theirs alone.

In the South they have an endearing habit, heavy lorries and smaller vehicles alike, of pulling over onto the hard shoulder to let faster traffic overtake in comfort. But there is a marked reluctance to dip headlights in the face of on-coming motorists at night.

Petrol costs are much higher in the Republic than in Northern Ireland, where they remain roughly in line with British prices. To complicate matters, quantities are now usually reckoned in litres in the South, and at present run at between IR56.8 and IR57.6 per litre, depending on grade. Much cheaper to hire a bicycle on arrival, and for those so inclined all-inclusive cycling holidays may be booked at prices which, including accommodation at youth hostels, range from about IR£40.00 per week. It is of course cheaper still to walk, and long-distance walking routes extending all over the country have been comprehensively mapped. They are documented in individual leaflets issued by the Irish Tourist Board, and may be used in conjunction with the excellent little county-by-county booklets that sell at IR50p each.

Whether feet or wheels bear the brunt of transport, it is important for the traveller to realise that major signs in the Republic now give distances in kilometres. Divide by three and multiply the result by two to get an approximate equivalent in miles.

Car Hire
Heavy insurance costs and the imposition of VAT at a punitive rate make car rental unnaturally high in southern Ireland, with the minimum charge for a Ford Fiesta, or a Mini Metro being reckoned at about £25.00 per day. Avis and Hertz and a number of local firms have offices in the principal cities, and by far the best of the latter group is Boland's-Inter Rent, a family organisation which holds an impeccable record for reliability and personal helpfulness.

Visitors bringing their own cars to Ireland need registration book and licence, a country identification plate and insurance certificate. Although under EEC regulations a Green Card is not required, it is advisable to confirm this with the insurance company concerned before setting off, and certainly some firms demand extra insurance for foreign cars visiting the Republic. 'Control Zones' in Northern Ireland mean that a car may not be left unattended; while in Dublin, where parking is a cruel problem, it is worth knowing that the reciprocal facilities that obtain between the RAC Club and Dublin's RIAC include private parking.

Taxis
The bigger cities have taxis, which may be hired from stationary ranks or summoned by telephone, but again costs need watching. Dublin, alas, is notorious for the high proportion of meters that fail to maintain working order for any length of time, while in Belfast two of the city's several taxi firms are affiliated to rival political organisations and ply their own chosen routes and none other. This is particularly disconcerting for visitors from London who hail a familiar black cab and suggest an alternative destination to the one the driver has in mind. Outside the cities taxis may be hired from private hackney firms, but it is wise to discuss the fare before undertaking a journey.

Accommodation

Hotels; Bed-and-Breakfast

Both the Irish Tourist Board and the Northern Ireland Tourist Board have information offices scattered throughout the country, and accommodation may be booked ahead through these for the price of a telephone call — an invaluable service for the traveller touring without fixed plans. Accommodation ranges from luxury hotels, some of them converted castles and manor houses, to less grand establishments and simple bed-and-breakfast addresses. These last have proved one of the major successes of Irish tourism in both parts of the country. Inspected regularly by the tourist authorities, they are invariably clean and comfortable and warm, often including private bathroom facilities in a nightly price of around £10.00, sterling or Irish, per head. To a woman, the landladies of these establishments are friendly and hospitable souls who offer cups of tea or sometimes something stronger on arrival, and, without turning a hair, rise at whatever unearthly hour may suit the guest to dish up mighty breakfasts that would keep a trencherman going for a week.

Where hotels are concerned, it is encouraging to remember that the prices quoted in official brochures are the **maximum** the establishment is allowed to charge. Lower rates and concessions are often available, and it is worth enquiring before dismissing any of them on grounds of expense.

Farmhouses; Renting

Meanwhile farmhouses are proving especially popular for extended family sojourns. These last have proved particularly popular for family holidays: they suit the nature of the country and in terms of simple comfort, ample food and a pleasant domestic atmosphere are reckoned to give good value for money.

Private houses may also be hired as holiday homes, and in some areas there are thatched cottages, purpose-built for the self-catering tourist. These lean heavily on the traditional in appearance and decoration, but are equipped with central heating and modern cooking facilities.

Camping; Youth Hostels

Camping, caravanning and youth-hostelling are catered for by sites and hostels in various parts of the country, and there is a mobile Irish speciality in the horse-drawn, gypsy-style caravan. Like the self-catering thatched cottages, these are more comfortably appointed than the traditional prototype, but remain all the same suitable strictly for lovers of the simple life — and of a really slow rate of progress to boot.

Currency

Ireland is no longer in the sterling area, and although the exchange rate varies slightly from time to time, the British £ is usually worth a few pence more than the Irish. Many places in the Republic still accept British currency as well as Irish, but are unlikely to offer more than face value in exchange. In Northern Ireland local currency has the same value as British.

Dollars are welcomed North and South, and often accepted in direct payment; travellers' cheques in either dollars or sterling will also be accepted in payment of sizeable bills by shops and hotels. Anyone from the EEC may cash personal cheques at a bank on production of a current Eurocard.

Customs and Immigration

Visitors from the US may bring with them 2½ lbs. of tobacco, ½ gallon of spirits, two bottles of wine and a pint of perfume or toilet water; EEC regulations obtain for European visitors. Domestic pets may be brought only from Britain, the Channel Islands and the Isle of Man but, as agriculture is the prime industry, there is a strict ban on the importation of meat, poultry and dairy products.

There are no passport formalities between Britain and Ireland. US citizens need a passport for entry to either country.

Duty-free shops at Irish and British airports are now open to travellers between Britain and the Republic, as well as to visitors from the Continent and the United States. However, by one of those extraordinary anomalies that are such an integral part of the fabric of Irish life, there are no duty-free concessions between Northern Ireland and the South. Traffic between the two parts of the country is unrestricted provided motorists keep to approved roads of access, and these are thoroughly documented by the Northern Ireland Tourist Board.

Diplomatic Representation

About 30 countries, including most of Europe, the United States, Canada, Japan, the Soviet Union and Australia, support embassies or consulates in Ireland, while as many more again have non-resident representation.
UK Embassy: 33 Merrion Road, Dublin 4
US Embassy: 42 Elgin Road, Dublin 4
US Consulate: Queen's House, Queen Street, Belfast.

Dress

The cardinal rule is: carry a raincoat, and bring some woollies along as well, for temperatures are variable. After that normal European standards prevail, though the Irish tend to more casual southern habits. Except in very grand establishments a man may sit down to dinner without a tie, and though formal clothes are usually worn for smart occasions at the theatre, sweaters and jeans are rarely turned away — unless of course a strictly-worded invitation has been issued.

Etiquette

This is relaxed and easy-going. The Irish are friendly souls with a genuine interest in other people and other people's ways: they fall happily into conversation with strangers, and as a mark of courtesy tend to ask direct questions which in other countries might be deemed inquisitive. In Ireland this is a sign of real concern, and if the answer to the inevitable question about what the visitor thinks of Ireland is carefully couched, chance acquaintance can ripen into friendship with invitations to spend an evening at the other's home or to come and meet new Irish friends at the pub next day.

The sincere wish to please, to be liked and to give visitors a good time carries a rather piquant backlash; for when the visitor in turn asks questions, the replies are likely to be based on what the informant **thinks** he would wish to hear. The classic example of this is the tired driver stopping to inquire the distance to the next town and being consoled with the news that it is only a few miles down the road — when in fact it is three or four times that. Grains of salt should be added to information of this kind.

Festivals and Entertainment

There is hardly a town or village in Ireland without a festival. Some are laid on to keep visitors entertained during the season; others, like the Wexford Opera Festival, are important cultural events in their own right. Meanwhile, throughout the country there are fairs, agricultural shows and gymkhanas, all with serious intent but at the same time engendering the party spirit in which Ireland excels. Most towns and villages have at least one cinema and a dance-hall, but nightclubs in the European sense are rare.

Food and Drink

Although there is no long-standing tradition of gastronomy in Ireland, the best of its hotels and restaurants are rapidly developing a fine national table based on superb raw materials — oysters, lobsters, mussels, scallops, salmon and white fish; excellent beef, ham and lamb. Only an enterprising few, however, can be persuaded to include traditional dishes like Irish Stew and boiled bacon-and-cabbage on their menus, and it is even more difficult to find these hearty and delicious staples of the private home in lesser catering establishments. All the more pity, as those few who make a point of including at least some traditional recipes on the menu have found them popular with visitors. The restaurant at the *Three Lakes Hotel* in Killarney, and *Sheila's* a few yards away, are both good examples.

Whatever the scarcity of local dishes, however, the marvellous home-made bread is available everywhere. Known as 'soda bread' to foreigners, it is called simply 'brown bread' by the Irish who use the former expression for another excellent bread-cake made with white flour. Both should be tried. In Northern Ireland, where every household seems to bake its own bread, the delicious alchemy is worked with wheaten flour instead of wholemeal, and in this part of the country there is also a devastating tradition of serving potato cakes with breakfast — irresistible ruin for waistlines.

It is hard to eat well and cheaply in the Republic. The good restaurants are very good indeed, but hideously expensive, while at the other end of the scale, the fare leans heavily on packaged soups, overcooked meat, watery vegetables and the ubiquitous fast food. Fortunately, there are encouraging signs of improvement in the middle price-range, and a relatively recent and very welcome development in belated recognition of the great bounty that lies in the sea, the lakes and the rivers. Fish has at last come into its own on Irish menus, and is nearly always of excellent quality and imaginatively cooked.

Another welcome innovation is the introduction of a special 'Tourist Menu' designed to ease the strain on holiday budgets. This provides good value in three-course meals at IR£5.60 or IR£7.50 at specified times of day, and while evening service may finish rather early for average adult taste, it has proved a godsend for families travelling with small children. Restaurants serving the 'Tourist Menu' are listed in the Irish Tourist Board's guide to eating out in Ireland, and in these and almost every other restaurant in the country it is still customary to offer tea as well as coffee at the end of a meal — which, given the price of alcohol in Ireland, may prove to be the only feasible choice for drinking with dinner.

Eating times are flexible in Ireland. Lunch is generally served from midday until 1500 and sometimes later, and in the cities cafés and short-order grills serve meals according to a restricted menu throughout the day. In Dublin there are enough late-night restaurants to ensure a meal after the theatre and well on into the early hours of the morning, but it is advisable to book in advance.

Drink
Until quite recently Ireland had a distinguished name for clarets — possibly dating from old connections with families who fled to France and in time became proprietors of vineyards: the 'Lynch' of Lynch-Bages and the 'Phélan' ('Whelan') of Phélan-Segur are both said to be of Irish origin. For decades there were remarkable cellars to be investigated in hotels and restaurants, while rare vintages often turned

up in unassuming little places, served simply as 'red wine' and incredibly underpriced.

Heavy taxation, plus an increasing national interest in wine, have altered this pleasant picture beyond belief, and alcoholic drinks now tend to be as expensive in Ireland as anywhere else, much more so in the Republic. The shock of paying IR£3.60 for a couple of gin-and-tonics in a middling-to-fair Dublin hotel may be tempered by the realisation that Irish measures are almost double the English, but there is no denying the punitive cost of table wines. An enterprising group of hoteliers and restaurateurs in Kinsale, where there is a gourmet festival every year, is investigating the possibility of buying a reasonable house wine in common to keep prices down, but elsewhere prospects are bleak. Even in an off-licence it is difficult to find a *vin ordinaire* of passable quality for less than £5.50.

The price of beer also causes the average English pint drinker to blench, and in fact, there is little variety in the beer in Ireland where the general choice is Guinness, either draught or bottled. It is said to taste better in Ireland than anywhere else in the world, and best of all in its home town of Dublin, the latter claim being hotly disputed by every other town and village in the country.

Irish gin and vodka are similar to those made in Britain, but Irish whiskey is a pot-still and has a distinctive taste, quite different from Scotch; Paddy has the most pronounced flavour of all, and connoisseurs will argue the toss between this and the merits of Jameson, Powers and Bushmills for hours. Irish whiskey is always used for Irish Coffee, a mixture of coffee, sugar and whiskey, topped with cream, and suitable only for the sweetest palates.

Genealogy

American visitors of Irish extraction are frequently fired with a passion to trace their ancestry when they set foot in Ireland, and there are several agencies whose function is research of this nature. A booklet listing the members of the Association of Professional Genealogists in Ireland is available from the Genealogical Office at 2 Kildare Street in Dublin.

Gratuities

Most hotels and restaurants now include a compulsory 10 per cent service charge, though this is sometimes as high as 12 or 15 per cent. No further gratuities are expected after that, though they will rarely be turned away.

Health

All visitors from EEC are entitled to medical treatment in Ireland. UK visitors should obtain an SA 28/July 1978 leaflet from their local social security offices before travelling, while those from elsewhere in the EEC need Form E111. The eight regional health boards will provide panels of doctors on request.

Language

Although a few communities in the Republic still speak Irish amongst themselves, English is the common language, and those whose mother-tongue is Irish are always bilingual. Road signs in the Republic are printed in both Irish and English.

Lavatories

Most towns of any size have segregated public conveniences for men and women. Their condition varies from place to place, and can be decidedly less than appealing on market days. Throughout the country, however, innkeepers and hoteliers are flexible about passers-by making use of their toilet facilities and this is invaluable for those touring in remote areas where amenities are few and far between. It might be wise to learn that *Fir* means 'Men' and *Mná* means 'Women', though to be fair there is usually a pictograhic illustration for the edification of anyone illiterate in both languages.

Maps

These are legion, and a good selection may be found in the leading bookshops of most of the bigger towns and cities. Ordnance survey maps of half-inch to a mile and quarter-inch to a mile cost about IR£2.70 each. Most good bookshops carry an immense selection of tourist literature and serious books about the country, and some of this is also available through Irish Tourist Board outlets.

National Parks and Walking Routes

There are several fine National Parks in Ireland, the most famous being Glenveagh in County Donegal, Killarney and Connemara. In addition long-distance walking paths have been designed through the most picturesque regions of the country, and leaflets describing these are available at local Tourist Offices. In principal, they keep to lesser and often unpaved routes and frequently cross private lands. The relevant leaflets give information about features of interest on the way, accommodation and general conditions likely to be encountered.

Post Offices and Police Stations

These are obvious in big towns, though in Northern Ireland the police stations are so heavily fortified that the man in the street thinks twice before trying to gain access. In rural areas in the Republic the green post office sign is sometimes so inconspicuous as to be wholly unnoticeable as it hangs outside an otherwise anonymous country cottage. Postal rates in Northern Ireland are the same as the UK. In the Republic a letter to Britain and other countries in the EEC costs IR28p; a postcard, IR24p.

The Pub

This is the pivot of social life in Ireland, and if the company is male the only inflexible rule is that those who stand a drink should be stood one in their turn. It is unlikely that a lone woman will be allowed to stand a round, though the days when unescorted women were unwelcome in Irish pubs have passed. At most in really remote areas women will be directed to a private room known as the 'parlour' and served there, but this is as much to save their blushes as the publican's; elsewhere women are accepted at the bar, though preferably in the lounge if there is one, while in the few rough pubs that still exist a lone woman is as liable to be subject to curiosity and harmlessly ribald gallantry as she would in a similar establishment anywhere else in the world.

Pubs in the Republic are open from 1000 until 2300 in winter, 2330 in summer — except in Dublin and Cork where enforced closing from 1430 to 1530 is known as the 'holy hour' but none too piously observed. Sunday opening times are from 1230 to 1400 and from 1600 to 2200. In Northern Ireland the pubs are open from 1100 to 2300 on weekdays, and follow British custom on Sunday. In both parts of the island hotel residents are entitled to order drinks at any time — though it is doubtful if the night porter of any small establishment, north or south of the border, will accept a request for drinks at three o'clock in the morning with much enthusiasm.

Public Holidays

The following public holidays are the same in the Republic and in Northern Ireland: Christmas Day and Boxing Day, December 25 and 26, also December 27: Good Friday and Easter Monday: St Patrick's Day, March 17. Northern Ireland has holidays on July 12 for Orange Day and on the last Monday in August for the Summer Bank Holiday. Other bank holidays in the Republic are Whit Monday in late May or early June, the first Monday in August for the Summer Bank Holiday and the final Monday in October.

Religion

Both the Roman Catholic church and the Protestant Church of Ireland are well represented on both sides of the Border, and minor Christian sects usually have at least a single seat of worship in major cities. The more exotic faiths from outside Europe do not fare as well but, with increasing interest in comparative religions, it is worth while at least making enquiries, and even if there is not a mosque conveniently to hand there is never any problem about making obeisance to the East.

Security

In common with the rest of Europe, Ireland has its share of violence, some might say more than its share. But outside the cities the country is generally quiet and safe for visitors. All the same, it is wise, particularly in big towns not to carry large sums of money or valuables, not to leave handbags carelessly disposed even in first-class hotels, and never, ever, to leave a car unlocked in any part of the country.

Shopping

The shops are open from 0930 to 1730 in big towns and cities, though in smaller places the general store often remains open until late in the evening. Saturday is the usual half-day, though some country towns close early on Thursday instead.

Irish linens and tweeds, traditional knitwear, lace and crochet are, together with Waterford glass, the most popular buys. A recent resurgence of interest in Celtic design is also resulting in fine ornaments and souvenirs of wood, silver, copper and enamel. Green Connemara marble is used for jewellery, ornaments and ashtrays, and is very attractive when not embellished with paste glitter. Another good buy is Irish smoked salmon, vacuum-packed for travelling, and in some country places it is still possible to find 'farmer's butter': lavishly smeared on the local brown bread, it makes an epicurean accompaniment to oysters, cold lobster or smoked salmon.

Sport

It is said that Ireland has the highest number of golf links per capita in the world, and many of them are championship courses.

Horses: Racing and Riding
The horse is even more dearly prized — on the racecourse, hacking gently along a country road or leaping the ditches and stone walls in one of the several hunts which are famous throughout Europe. Ireland has plenty of riding schools, and the Irish Tourist Board publishes a leaflet with information about the hunts. There is good shooting, too, though this is strictly controlled for obvious reasons.

Fishing
For its size Ireland provides better, cheaper and more plentiful game and coarse fishing than anywhere else in the world. There is good sea-angling, too, and the Republican and Northern Ireland tourist

boards have thoroughly documented all the fishing grounds, plus their minimal charges, rules and restrictions. Enquiries at any of their offices will produce a vast assortment of literature on the subject.

Water Sports
The long, wandering Irish coastline has countless, vast sandy beaches with nearly always safe bathing, and outside towns and popular resorts a low rate of occupancy. There is excellent sailing off the coast, while inland lie some 800 lakes and rivers.

Other water sports in Ireland include canoeing and wind-surfing, while strategically situated throughout the country are a number of 'activity centres' which cater for the growing enthusiasm for adventure sports.

Cruising
Recent years have seen the development of the Shannon, the Barrow and Lough Erne for cabin cruisers, and these provide one of the most enjoyable holidays imaginable. The waterways are vast and endlessly interesting in their scenery, wild life and angling opportunities, and in the evenings the little towns and villages along the shore explode into lively social activity as the boats come in to moor and their crews descend on the pubs. Several companies operate cruiser fleets for hire, one of the best being Emerald Star Line which has its head-quarters at St James's Gate, Dublin. Visitors bringing their own boats to Ireland may travel by the Grand Canal from Dublin to explore the River Barrow or, if keel dimensions are suitable, continue on to the Shannon.

Spectator Sport
Amongst spectator sports the most important is the national game of hurling. Fast and exciting, it is played with sticks and a ball and inspires extraordinary feats of speed and skill from participants. Kilkenny and Wexford are the traditional champions of the game and may frequently be seen locked in spectacular combat for the All-Ireland Hurling Final at Dublin's Croke Park.

Tourist Offices
In Ireland:
Irish Tourist Board: Baggot Street Bridge, Dublin 2; tel. 765871 and 616500.
Northern Ireland Tourist Board: 48 High Street, Belfast, BT1 2DS; tel. 321221.

Overseas:
UK: Irish Tourist Board, 150 New Bond Street, London W1Y 0AQ; tel. 01 493 3201.
Northern Ireland Tourist Board, 11 Berkeley Street, London W1X 6BU; tel. 01 493 0601.

USA: Irish Tourist Board, 757 Third Avenue, New York, NY 10017;
tel. 212 418 0800.
Northern Ireland Tourist Board, 40 West 57th Street, 3rd Floor,
New York, NY 10019; tel. 212 765 5144.

All these offices are happy to assist potential visitors with information and advice, though bookings must be handled directly by travel agents, carriers or other commercial interests. But once the tourist has arrived and started travelling in the country, by far the most valuable manifestations of the national tourism authorities are the Tourist Information Offices scattered about the country. Eighteen of these operate throughout the year, but there are many more in action during the summer. All of them are helpful, most of them are staffed by charmers, but there is none the equal of the Tourist Information Office in Westport, County Mayo. Thank you, Mary.

Clonmacnoise, Co. Offaly

History and Culture

The Island

Ireland is the westernmost island of the European continental shelf. It measures 32,524 square miles and no part of the country is more than seventy miles from the sea. There are thirty-two counties in all, six of them comprising the British province of Northern Ireland and the remaining twenty-six administered from Dublin by the Government of the Irish Republic. The chapters of this book are divided according to the historic provinces of Leinster, Munster, Connacht and Ulster, with an extra section devoted to those counties in every province which are drained by the River Shannon and form the lakelands of Ireland.

The population of Ireland was drastically reduced by the great famine of the 19th century and its aftermath, and has never recovered its former strength. It is now about 3.5 million in the Republic, and over a million and a half in Northern Ireland — which leaves plenty of open country for the traveller: uncrowded roads, empty beaches, uncongested towns, and everywhere room to move about at leisure. A rapid tour of Ireland could be made in ten or twelve days by keeping to the coast, but three weeks is a more feasible estimate for comfortable travelling. It would take about three months to explore the country thoroughly; a lifetime, its enthusiasts claim, to know it intimately.

The central limestone plain of Ireland contains large areas of bog, deposits of sand and clay, and several hundred lakes. Around this the coast rises in highlands and mountains of different geological composition: red standstone rock in the south and south-west, limestone and shale going north along the west coast, in the west itself a mixture of granite, quartzite and volcanic rock, and in the north-east a great basalt plateau. The Mountains of Mourne and Carlingford are of granite, while a more extensive granite region is formed by the Wicklow Mountains to the south of Dublin.

The effects of the Ice Age are very marked in Ireland, particularly in Kerry with its glacial valleys, while the Gulf Stream ameliorates the climate to a mildness which encourages the growth of plants more commonly associated with southern Europe. Rainfall is high, except in the south-east, largely unpredictable and responsible for the deep overall green colour of the countryside. May, June, August and September are generally reckoned to be the driest and sunniest months, but there is no telling in advance.

History

Early Irish history is an unfathomable blend of fact and fantasy — based on the eminently tangible evidence of prehistoric stone, but taking off from there in great epic legends which have the status of classical mythology and may well have equal relevance to real events. Later history, from the coming of the Normans onwards, is so well documented that any attempt to pot it is liable to charges of oversimplification and inaccuracy. For the superficial purposes of most visitors, one of the best and most evocative potted versions may be seen at the Ulster Museum in Belfast.

Stone Age to the Celts
It is generally agreed that man arrived in Ireland during the Stone Age, about 6000 BC. The glaciers of the Ice Age had retreated by then, and the first settlers used flint for hunting and domestic chores. From this period onwards successive waves of immigrants arrived from the east, each new invasion accompanied by more sophisticated concepts of living; and the building of the huge stone tombs and burial courts increased to such an extent that the uninformed observer might well assume prehistoric Ireland to have been simply a vast necropolis.

History and Culture

This was not the case of course for, whatever else his beliefs, primitive man was keenly concerned with survival after death: his tombs were built to last, his mortal dwelling recognised as such and so long since vanished. A few *crannógs*, which possibly date from neolithic times, have been identified: these were small artificial islands built as dwelling centres and probably defended by wooden pallisades. There is one at Lough Gur in County Limerick and at Graggaunowen in Co. Clare, near a 15th-century tower housing a collection of Celtic and mediaeval artefacts, a conjectural reconstruction includes a lake dwelling of wattle-and-reed, an Iron Age ring fort and also the hide-skin vessel in which more recently Tim Severin repeated the voyage to the New World made by St Brendan the Navigator some 1,500 years ago.

The first settlers, whose origins are much disputed, were the Nemedians, and in time they were vanquished by Formorian pirates. Then came the Firbolgs, and then the Tuatha Dé Danann — with whom the legends really start. Tribes of the goddess, Dana, they practised magic, and when the Milesians came, their art availed to enable them survive as fairy people underground. To this day farmers in remote districts are reluctant to disturb a 'fairy ring', whatever the exigencies of modern husbandry.

The Milesians were Celts of Spanish origin, and became in historical terms the indigenous population of the country. A recognisable European pattern of small kingdoms under a central overlordship emerged, accompanied by the evolution of a warrior aristocracy. The Romans in Britain thought that a single legion would be enough to subdue the Irish, but the Celts had their wits about them and the High King, Cormac Mac Art, founded the *Fianna*, a band of professional warriors under the leadership of Fionn Mac Cumhail, to discourage any territorial ambitions their neighbours to the east might have. In the event the invasion never came, and hoards of Roman gold discovered in Northern Ireland are attributed to forays by the Irish into Britain, rather than the other way round.

The High Kings and Christianity
The power of the high King was vested at Tara in County Meath, and his court included lawyers, poets, bards and druids as distinct and formal social classes. There is a good deal of speculation and scepticism about the druids and their nastiness, with later theories firmly discounting earlier rumours of child sacrifice. Whatever the truth of the matter, the arrival of St Patrick in the 5th century put a stop to it.

Legend has it that he was the son of a Roman Officer in Britain; was taken in a raid by Niall of the Nine Hostages — whose descendants ruled in Ulster up to the 17th century — and spent his youth as a slave tending sheep on the hillsides of Antrim. The isolated circumstances of such a life were conducive to the reception of heavenly voices and, on their instruction, the future saint ran away and escaped from Ireland on a boat carrying wolfhounds to the Continent. After a period of monastic apprenticeship at Auxerre, he returned and does not seem to have encountered much opposition in his conversion of the heathen Irish to Christianity.

The new faith spread rapidly through the country, and by the time the Vikings appeared towards the end of the 8th century, Ireland was a holy place, widely respected as the 'Island of Saints and Scholars'. Its monasteries were legion, celebrated centres of piety and learning where literature was kept alive while the Dark Ages raged in Europe. From that period dates the Irish missionary tradition which is still vigorous in the 20th century: from Ireland St Colmcille — who is also known as St Columba — sailed off to convert the Picts of Iona, and St Columbanus to found monasteries in France, Germany and Italy.

Vikings to Normans
Meanwhile the Vikings had begun their fierce plundering, the shallow draught of their longboats enabling them to penetrate inland to raid and despoil the monasteries. This led to the building of the Round Towers, which are still a typical feature of the Irish countryside: their doors were ten or twelve feet above the ground so that when a Norse fleet was sighted, the monks could scramble up a rope ladder, haul it after them and sit out the raid in safety.

The Vikings established settlements along the Irish coast, notably at Dublin, Wexford, Waterford and Cork, and at Limerick on the mouth of the Shannon. These became important commercial centres, and the influence of Tara began to decline — until early in the 11th century when a Munster soldier-king called Brian Boru succeeded in unifying the country and in 1014 defeated the Norsemen for good and all at the Battle of Clontarf. He was killed the same day by a fugitive from the battlefield, and with his death the kings of Connacht came to the fore.

The O'Connor kings, however, failed to impose a strong centralised leadership, so that within a hundred years Ireland had degenerated into a conglomeration of dissenting rulers, far too preoccupied with internal squabbles to take serious note of the formidable new society rising on the other side of the Irish Sea. The king of Leinster, Dermot MacMurrough, ran off with Dervorgilla, wife of Tiernan O'Rourke of Breiffne, and when the latter's ally, Rory O'Connor, became High King, the deserted husband seized the opportunity to unseat his rival. The deposed monarch sailed for Bristol seeking help to regain his throne and offering his handsome daughter, Eva, in marriage to whoever would take up his cause. The Earl of Pembroke, known as 'Strongbow', jumped at the bargain and in 1169 the Norman conquest of Ireland began with Welsh and Fleming volunteers.

Normans to the Reformation
There is no doubt that the Normans would have invaded Ireland sooner or later. They had been entrenched in Britain for over a century, and were eager for further territorial expansion; and they had the military and administrative skill to accomplish it. But in Irish memory the blame lies exclusively with Dermot, and thereby does him too much honour.

Strongbow's armies had taken the principal cities by 1171, when Henry II arrived, authorised by an ancient Papal Bull to restore the Irish Church to the path of orthodoxy from which it had comfortably meandered in the preceeding autonomous centuries. The king was also anxious to assert his sovereignty over Strongbow's obvious dominance in Ireland, and to ensure succession for his son who later became King John.

Many of the Irish submitted to Henry II in the hope of securing their lands, but the Normans continued to make heavy inroads on the country — and then by process of assimilation to adopt the customs of the conquered. They wore Irish dress and long Irish hairstyles and began to exhibit sympathies to match; by the time the Statutes of Kilkenny, forbidding fraternisation with the Irish, were passed in the 14th century, the great Norman family of Fitzgerald, which had an earldom in Kildare and another in the Desmond territory of Munster, was an almost invincible bulwark of Gaelic civilisation. It was to the 'Geraldines' that the O'Neills of Ulster, who had somehow managed to retain their overlordship of the north inviolate, sent for support in their wars with the English in the 16th century.

Had it not been for the Reformation, it is possible that Ireland might eventually have settled down as a contented Anglo-Irish society under the titular sovereignty of the English crown. Resistance to the rules of the Reformation was fierce, but Henry VIII proved stronger, and the repression he initiated was continued by his daughter with the first of the plantations which were to change the whole structure of society in Ireland. A few years after the decisive Battle of Kinsale, which took place in 1601, the O'Neill and O'Donnell chiefs sailed away for ever and their estates in the north were handed over to planters.

Cromwell to Emancipation
Things went from bad to worse during the Civil War in England. Siding with Charles I, a Catholic Confederate army secured several victories in Ireland, but Cromwell's arrival with 20,000 men was too much for the defenders, and the Protector underlined his stern, inflexible resolve by massacring the best part of the populations of Drogheda and Wexford. Only at Clonmel, where a remaining scion of the O'Neill family was in command, were the Cromwellians defeated.

In 1690 the pattern was repeated, though hardly with such ferocity, as James II made a last stand in Ireland: he lost to William of Orange at the Battle of the Boyne, and a year later the fall of Limerick left Ireland open to the implementation of severe Penal Laws which deprived Roman Catholics of most of their political and educational freedom.

It was too much to hope that repressive policies of this magnitude would succeed in a country where religion and political freedom were becoming synonymous. The American War of Independence promoted a national consciousness which within a century had been transmuted into conscious nationalism, and the French Revolution proved that established order could be overthrown. In 1790 Wolfe Tone founded the United Irishmen who launched an insurrection eight years later; although it failed, despite a brief and bloody success in Wexford, it was this movement which resulted in the first coherent idea of republicanism.

In 1800, too late to destroy the seeds Wolfe Tone had planted, the Dublin parliament was abolished and Irish members took their seats at Westminster instead. It was there that Daniel O'Connell, a dema-gogic lawyer known as the 'Liberator', secured substantial measures of relief for Irish Catholics. As a Catholic himself, O'Connell was barred from taking his seat when he was elected to Parliament in 1826, but it was obvious to the Duke of Wellington, then Prime Minister and also an Irishman, that liberal winds were blowing, and within two years the Emancipation Bill was law.

The Famine; the Easter Rising
The great famine of the mid-19th century brought Ireland to its lowest condition ever. Mismanagement cruelly exacerbated its effects, and by the time it was over, starvation and a panic wave of emigration had reduced the population by a quarter. Emigration continued over the next fifty years, while those who remained behind campaigned for land reform and home rule. By the end of the century a republican movement, strongly supported by Irish emigrants in America, was gathering force for the events that culminated in the Easter Rising of 1916.

initially, there was not much sympathy amongst the general public for the Rising, but feeling changed dramatically with the prompt execution of most of its leaders. For the next five years *Sinn Fein* campaigned throughout the country, winning local elections whole-sale but refusing to sit at Westminster and instead in 1919 instituting its own parliament, the first *Dáil Eireann*. A stubborn policy of guerilla warfare harassed the forces of the Crown meanwhile, and in 1921 Lloyd George suggested a truce for negotiation. The agreement according the twenty-six counties which now form the Irish Republic dominion status under the Crown was signed the same year with the

27

proviso that the six counties of Northern Ireland should not be forced to join them.

The Treaty was accepted by the majority of the *Dáil* in Dublin, but dissident republicans refused to settle for anything short of total independence for the whole country. Civil war followed. It lasted about six months and set up political allegiances which survive to this day, but in the end the moderate supporters of the 'Free State' won, and Ireland did not become a republic until 1949. The former dissident Eamon de Valera, ended his days as its president.

The Republic and Northern Ireland

Events since then have seen considerable advances towards economic prosperity and political maturity in the Republic; in Northern Ireland a dreadful schism between the Protestant and Roman Catholic factions of the population. The roots of this problem are so deeply embedded in history that no one outside the province can possibly understand them, and perhaps not many within do either. At present the situation seems to be insoluble, with both sides irrevocably in the wrong, and the only hope is that membership of the EEC, plus the affluence that must ultimately accrue from it, will bring about mutual tolerance in time.

Meanwhile the much-publicised violence remains localised, and visitors to Northern Ireland will see little evidence of it outside acknowledged trouble spots. Instead there is a countryside of tranquil lakes and mountains, of ancient castles and quiet villages, of soft-spoken friendly people whose droll sense of humour indicates that the present crisis must somehow be overcome by common sense in the end.

Language, Art, Folk Culture

Language

The past remains as vivid as the present in the minds of many Irishmen, and they are happy to talk about Ireland, and the condition of being Irish, for hours on end. The more fervent perform this feat in Irish.

Far more efficiently than English repression, the famine annihilated the common use of the native language in Ireland, and its revival was a natural vehicle for rising nationalism around the turn of the century. Since Ireland became self-governing the urgent promotion of national identity has hardly been necessary and the Irish-language revival has degenerated into a bludgeon in the service of political opportunists, professional and otherwise. Lip-service is exacted, quite literally at times, from the most unlikely victims, while romanisation of the alphabet and oversimplification of the old spelling provide a source of mixed amusement and irritation in the few surviving native-speaking communities. These are described collectively as the *Gaeltacht*. Their people regard the veneration with which earnest revivalists approach them with healthy cynicism and make no bones about speaking excellent English with the rest of the world.

For the visitor, however, the influence of Irish is more interesting than its practice — for the centuries when Irish was the language of the majority of the population have given English, as spoken in Ireland, an extra dimension of eloquence and lyricism. This is immediately apparent in the work of such dramatists as Synge and O'Casey and, for those who listen to how people speak as well as what they say, equally striking in everyday speech throughout the country. Some expressions are direct translations from Irish — which is different from English in both construction and form — and there is a pleasure in using words, and lots of them, for their own sake, which finds a ready outlet in writing.

Literature
In the past the economic structure of Ireland was hardly propitious to the development of such potentially expensive cultural forms as art and music. Imagination, however, costs nothing, and from the 18th century onwards Ireland produced an impressive volume of writers, not all of them deriving inspiration directly from their native heritage, but to a man gifted with powerful fancy and fluency. Before this time the literature of the country was in Irish and tended more to lyric poetry than prose, though the ancient epic sagas survived in manuscripts of the 12th century such as the 'Book of the Dun Cow' and the 'Book of Leinster', and in the 'Yellow Book of Lecan' which dates from the 14th/15th century

Music
Symphonic evolution is a costly process, and music in Ireland did not develop in the European manner. Composers such as John Field, who invented the nocturne as a musical form, and Balfe, whose operas were the rage of 19th-century Europe, found success abroad, while at home old airs, derived originally from the bardic system, continued to be sung with harp or fiddle accompaniment; later many of them found their way, in somewhat emasculated shape, into Victorian drawing rooms. The itinerant harpist vanished towards the end of the 18th century, but the great Belfast Harp Festival of 1792 moved collectors to tour the country taking down the old tunes which might otherwise have been lost for ever.

The establishment of radio orchestras in the present century has given sharp impetus to conventional music in Ireland, and there are now composers working in the sophisticated idiom of the contemporary world. Far more widespread, however, is the rivival of folk music, genuine and spurious, and the rise of the Irish ballad as a popular entertainment. Groups of young ballad-singers are as welcome at

History and Culture

private parties as they are in public houses, and any programme for visitors is apt to include at least one 'ballad evening' — which can be good fun, provided the performers do not take themselves too seriously and insist on the reverent hush appropriate to the formal concert hall.

Painting

Whatever the material circumstances of the individual involved, painting, like music, requires stable conditions of affluence and leisure. Lack of these deprived Ireland of normal development in the visual arts, and Irish taste remained unformed for centuries; and when at last it did begin to assume tangible shape was inevitably expressed in an inordinate passion for prettifying. A truly horrendous tradition of religious *kitsch* developed in ornamentation in churches and homes, followed in the present century by a wholesale addiction to plastic for secular decoration.

Things are changing rapidly for the better, however. The 20th century has seen several Irish painters and sculptors coming to prominence, and there is a growing recognition of the importance of design in private and public life. There is rich inspiration to be harvested from ancient Celtic material, and although it will be a while before the new spirit — which is surely one of the healthier manifestations of nationalism — realises its full potential, it is already a powerful and admirable force.

Castletown, Kildare

Leinster

Although Leinster covers a large area, extending as far west as the Shannon and from the extreme south-eastern tip of the country to the borders of Northern Ireland, it is the eastern segment which gives the province its character. This long coastal strip, with its substantial hinterland, corresponds to the heart of the former Pale — that reluctantly flexible centre of English administration which over the centuries waxed and waned in accordance with the fluctuating fortunes of the British within and the Irish without. A notable exception was County Wicklow where the wild and intransigent mountains remained virtually impenetrable for years and allowed the native O'Toole and O'Byrne clans to rampage almost at will.

The Pale has gone but its influence remains; and although they will thank no one for saying so, the people of east Leinster are more anglicised — or at least less overtly Gaelic, in their ways and culture than elsewhere in Ireland. This is, however, in part also a natural consequence of the land itself: largely arable and gentle, it invited

31

agriculture and social civilisation from the earliest times and reveals the cumulative result of these forces today. The stately homes of the region show the benign consequences of centuries of loving care, and in June several of them co-operate as hosts in a series of concerts to provide a festival of music in great Irish houses.

Those counties to the west of the province — Offaly, Westmeath and Longford— have a different character, and are dealt with in the section of this book devoted to the Shannon and the Lakelands.

County Dublin

Dublin

Dublin, which celebrated its millenium in 1988, is as much a state of mind as a city. Ever since James Joyce put them on the map as 'characters', Dubliners have been vain of their reputation as wits and writers and talkers and drinkers — though in fact they were known abroad for these qualities long before. Certainly the city has produced a vast number of brilliant writers — amongst them, Swift, Goldsmith, and Sheridan, Wilde, Shaw and Yeats, Sean O'Casey, James Joyce and Brendan Behan — though since St John Gogarty, it has lacked the private diarist it so richly deserves. For despite top-heavy, sprawling suburbs, Dublin retains its urban core intact — psychologically at least — and is perhaps the last remaining city in Europe where a latter-day Proust might flourish. There is prodigious material in the highly articulate and intellectually inbred Dublin society which feeds upon its own wits to devastatingly entertaining effect; in the endlessly interrelated cliques and coteries whose manipulation of gossip is a sophisticated exercise; in the talented turning of a malicious phrase, the seasoned appreciation of a scandal.

Not everyone succumbs to the slightly rackety charm of the city, or to the sharp-tongued humour of its people, but most visitors find them irresistible — and the Dublin pubs unique. The shabbier the pub, it seems, the better the talk will be, the more colourful the clientele and very likely, the finer the Guinness — which, it is generally conceded, tastes better in Dublin than anywhere else in the world. All the same the smarter establishments such as Davy Byrne's and the reconstituted Bailey (both of Joycean distinction), the Dawson Lounge and Neary's have plenty of local colour; and it would be a hard day's luck for any Dubliner to drop into one of these and fail to

Right: St. Patrick's Day Parade, Dublin
Royal Dublin Society Horse Show
Overleaf: The Fourcourts, Dublin

see at least a familiar face, if not a veritable nest of like-minded cronies eager to stand a round and be stood one in turn. The literati of the city gather frequently in the back bar of the old Clarence Hotel on Wellington Quay, while at coffee time a vivid cross-section of local society may be observed in either of Bewley's popular 'Oriental Cafés'. There is one in Grafton Street and another in Westmoreland Street.

Architecture
Although the city dates back to AD 140, its present design derives mainly from the spacious planning of the 18th century — when an Irish parliament sat in what is now the Bank of Ireland and Dublin was prosperous and elegant. It began to go downhill with the Act of Union in 1800, but there was no really dangerous decline in its good looks until the Easter Rising of 1916, when the British shelled the city from a gunboat on the River Liffey. During the Civil War which followed the setting up of the Free State, the Irish continued the destruction the enemy had begun, so that today nearly every important building reveals evidence of change and restoration.

For all that, the signs of re-building are in most cases blatant only to the architecturally-informed eye, and Gandon's glorious Custom House still rises serenely above the river without any obvious concession to restoration, although the view from a distance is masked by an excessively ugly railway bridge. All the more pity as the Custom House is balanced up-river by the sterner lineaments of Gandon's Four Courts, while the core of another Gandon design remains beneath the later wings and cupola of the King's Inns.

Bank of Ireland
The work of three different architects is represented by the vast, pillared pile of the Bank of Ireland which somehow, despite the successive stages of its making, still manages to form an impressive unity on its great, curving corner site. When the building was sold to the Bank the British Government insisted that the interior should be altered so that it might never again be suitable for parliamentary purposes; the old Lords' chamber still remains, however, and it seems a pity that the Irish Government did not decide to restore the building to its original function.

Leinster House, Trinity College
Instead the new rulers chose Leinster House, its central section built in 1745, its two great wings added later and now housing the National Museum on the south side, and on the north, the National Library

Previous page: The Gap of Dunloe, Killarney
Haymaking, Co. Cork
Left: Blarney Castle, near Cork
Georgian doorways, Dublin

and the National College of Art. Most of the extant treasures of ancient Ireland, from the Stone Age onwards, may be seen in the National Museum and the volume is considerable. The National Library has a large collection of valuable manuscripts, while many more are distributed between the Royal Irish Academy, Marsh's Library, which dates from the very beginning of the 18th century, and of course Trinity College which holds the great Book of Kells and the Book of Durrow, two famous manuscripts from early Christian times.

Trinity College itself is one of the most handsome buildings in the city, and is worth an extended visit. The great library, the dining-hall, the chapel and the examination hall are all basically 18th century, though not all untouched by the hand of time and the improver. The Provost's House remains completely unchanged, but is not open to the public.

Other important public buildings around the city include the Mansion House, the City Hall, the National Gallery, the Municipal Art Gallery, which occupies beautiful premises in Charlemont House, and Dublin Castle.

Dublin Castle
Dublin Castle, the bastion of British administration in Ireland for centuries, is rather disappointing to look at in its mixture of successive architectural styles but redeemed within by the State Apartments which now serve for the inauguration of Ireland's presidents. St. Patrick's Hall is a noble and spacious chamber with frescoes decorating its lofty ceiling, while the church in the Castle enclosure, formerly the Chapel Royal, has some fine examples of Irish oak carving.

The 18th century more or less peters out at Dublin Castle and the City Hall, and the earlier shape of the city emerges to the west in poor, haphazard streets and lanes, in the recently-restored Tailors' Hall, which is the only remaining guildhall in Dublin and, above all, in the ancient churches on both sides of the river.

Christ Church Cathedral
The days when Fishamble Street merited the first performance of the 'Messiah' have gone, but Christ Church Cathedral remains, the oldest building in Dublin rising gracefully above the river near the sole surviving arch of one of the old city walls.

It was built on the site of an earlier church by the conquering Norman Earl of Pembroke, dubbed Strongbow. Begun in 1172, it underwent many changes over the centuries, including major restoration in the 1870s, and today only the north and south transepts survive from the original 12th-century building — above ground that is, for the crypt running the length of the church is still intact and indeed was in use until quite recent times as a market place. Despite the changes Christ Church remains very beautiful, and a wonderful atmosphere lingers amongst its tall, elegant arches; it was always a focal point of Dublin life in the past, and in 1487 saw the coronation of the ten-year-old pretender, Lambert Simnel, as King of England. Strongbow himself is buried there, though there is some doubt about the authenticity of his supposed effigy in the nave.

Beside the old arch which once gave access to the city St Audeon's preserves a late 12th-century door and a peal of bells dating from the 15th century, while also in the immediate vicinity is St Werburgh's, built in the 12th century but much enlarged early in the eighteenth when it served as Dublin's parish church.

Viking Site
Below the cathedral, in one of the short street running down to the river, is the 'Brazen Head' which dates from 1688 and is almost certainly the oldest pub in Dublin. Near here Wood Quay exhibits a disgraceful monument to the perversity of the City Fathers in the shape of brash modern office blocks which have been built, in full knowledge and with criminal disregard for history and for public opinion, on top of a Viking site. There were massive protests against the proposed building when the layout of the ancient city appeared during excavations for the new foundations, but obtuse local authority prevailed at the cruel expense of remains believed to be unique in Europe.

St Patrick's Cathedral
Dublin has two cathedrals, neither of them Roman Catholic and both in the older part of the city, though St Patrick's was originally situated beyond the walls to evade subordination to the senior foundation of Christ Church.

Today it seems only a stone's throw away and forms a grey, dignified monument of tranquillity in the middle of a shabby urban area. Another 12th century foundation, it was extensively re-built after a fire in the 14th century and was the seat of a university until suppressed by Henry VIII during the Reformation. Much of the present building is due to 19th-century restoration, but again the memories of ages past remain almost tangible in its lofty, dark recesses: the banners of the Knights of St Patrick hang in forlorn pride from the walls, and amongst the commemorative plaques to great and well-known figures is one strange and inexplicable inscription to a hereditary standard-bearer of Montenegro.

Jonathan Swift was Dean of St Patrick's from 1713 until 1745, and both his grave and his beloved Stella's are in the cathedral. Irascible and witty, he was much concerned with the plight of Dublin's people and when he died left money to build a mental hospital in the

Leinster

neighbourhood — describing his own generous gesture wryly:

> *He gave the little wealth he had*
> *To build a house for fools and mad*
> *And showed by one satiric touch,*
> *No nation needed it so much.*

Guinness Brewery
St Patrick's Hospital still thrives with no apparent shortage of material, and in the same area is the great Guinness Brewery — which may or may not be coincidence. 'Uncle Arthur', as he is affectionately known to Dubliners has kept Ireland supplied with its favourite beverage for close on three centuries now, and a good part of the world outside as well. His hand, however, is set to more than one plough, for Guinness philanthropy is one of the more important civilising influences in Ireland, and is responsible for the preservation of many a precious building — St Patrick's Cathedral being an example — and the shoring-up of many a worthy but wobbly cultural enterprise. Sometime Guinness largesse is discreetly distributed, sometimes with much publicity and brouhaha, and sometimes it takes the form of personal action by a member of the family — as in the case of the Hon. Desmond Guinness's leadership of the Irish Georgian Society which maintains a steady and effective campaign to save the country's 18th-century heritage.

St Catherine's Church
The fount of all the good things, the brewery itself, however, stands in an undistinguished part of the city, relieved from drabness only by the façade of 18th-century St Catherine's Church which has been rescued from demolition to become an arts centre.

Kilmainham Hospital and Jail
Slightly further west the city reaches out to embrace Kilmainham with its ancient hospital and the extraordinarily poignant jail where the leaders of the 1916 Rising were executed. Both buildings have been restored, and the hospital is in much demand for functions. It is a striking example of classical Franco-Dutch design and contains splendid wood carvings, but the florid Caroline ceiling is only a replica of the original which collapsed in 1902. The clock tower dates from 1701.

Other Churches
In the centre Dublin's old churches continue across the river with St Michan's which dates mainly from the 17th century, although its tower is believed to be much earlier; some strange property of the vaults here has preserved the dead free from decomposition for centuries. Further north are a few fragments of 10th-century Mary's Abbey, then 17th-century St Mary's Church. About ten minutes' walk away is one of the few admirable 19th-century buildings in Dublin, the 'Black

Church'. This was built in 1830 and is a singularly unembellished and striking example of the Gothic Revival: aloof and dramatic, it stands in a small clear space, and it is said that the Devil runs around it three times at the stroke of midnight. There have been no reliable witnesses of this phenomenon to date.

The Quays; The Rotunda
The best way to savour the restless, lively atmosphere of Dublin is to walk. A new and possibly superficial affluence creates incongruous juxtapositions of gloss and shoddy at every hand's turn, but while inflation forces prices up beyond belief, no one seems to go seriously short.

The quays which line the River Liffey with unassuming but collectively picturesque old buildings lead into the centre of the city and divide it into south and north, the former fashionable, the latter not, for this route goes through wide and mercilessly commercialised O'Connell Street, past the GPO which was the centre of the 1916 Rising, to a sad network of decaying Georgian streets and squares beyond the Rotunda complex.

The Rotunda is believed to be the oldest maternity hospital in Europe, and its original mid-18th century heart contains a chapel with remarkable plasterwork. The neighbouring cinema occupies the former Rotunda Assembly Rooms, built at the same time as the hospital and intended to raise funds for it. Paganini was amongst those who played there and is said to have scattered gold coins to the ragamuffin children of the city as he drove away after his concert.

Between them, neglect and misguided development have ruined much of Dublin's good architecture on the north side — though the Irish Georgian Society is making a hard fight for the fine houses of Mountjoy Square — but there is still a substantial amount left on the south.

South of the Liffey
It starts with the shopping centre of Grafton Street and Dawson Street and their ancillary arcades; then Stephen's Green, though this has been sadly defaced by development on the south side, then Merrion Square and Street, Upper Mount Street (strangely in harmony with its 19th-century church known as the 'Pepper Cannister'), Fitzwilliam Street and Square — the former shamefully brutalised by the recent intrusion of really ugly modern offices — Baggot Street, Ely Place, some terraces along the Grand Canal, and much more. The Duke of Wellington, Oscar Wilde, Yeats and countless other famous Irishmen were either born or lived in the neighbourhood, and enough of its elegance remains to recapture something of the atmosphere of Dublin in those days. More important, there are encouraging signs that despite the ugly inroads of speculative building, and the short-sightedness of local authorities, today's Dubliners are beginning to

recognise the value of these treasures and are determined to save them from despoil. Meanwhile they serve as clubs, offices, shops, consulting rooms, cafés and flats, happily part of the integral fabric of Dublin life.

Theatre and Music

This life is a gregarious, sociable affair, with much visiting and entertaining and theatre-going, the last being a rather self-conscious passion deriving from the great days of Yeats and Synge and the Abbey Theatre. These days almost as much energy goes into the running battle to save the city's none-too-plentiful theatres from demolition or conversion, but fortunately the Abbey and the Gate — which under Hilton Edwards and Michael MaLiammóir made Dublin theatre truly international from the 1930s — remain inviolate, and prolific theatrical activity goes on in all sorts of halls and odd venues as well as in more formal premises. It has received considerable stimulus in recent years from the influx of writers attracted to the country by the Irish Government's tax concessions to creative artists: under this remarkable system all creative artistic work is exempt from tax — posing nice problems of distinction for those who administer the scheme, but none at all for those hoping to benefit by it.

The theatre season reaches its climax in September with the annual Dublin Theatre Festival, an event which has proved a springboard to the West End or Broadway for several playrights and even whole productions. Late drinking is permitted at the seasonal Theatre Club after the performances, and there are those who allege that there is more drama to be found at the club than in the theatre earlier in the evening. The former has, after all, the advantage of spontaneity.

Music is hardly as well served as theatre in Dublin, though under the distinguished professorship of Dr Anthony Hughes, the faculty of music at University College Dublin has done much to improve matters in recent years. Ireland now produces a substantial body of talented instrumentalists, and there are a number of Irish composers working in the modern idiom. There are regular concerts at the National Concert Hall throughout the year, chamber music and solo recitals in the library of the Royal Dublin Society and two seasons of grand opera in Dublin's Gaiety Theatre. A newly-established international piano competition has attracted a great deal of interest from abroad.

Horse-Racing

But horse-racing is a far more profound passion than any of the artistic disciplines, both here and in most other parts of the country, and there are enough courses and meets in and around Dublin to keep the citizens blissfully busy.

Restaurants

Whatever form of entertainment Dubliners choose, they are likely to end the day in a restaurant. These have multiplied in recent years and many of them stay open far later than is customary in northern Europe. This is one of the reasons Scandinavians, in particular, tend to regard the Irish as misplaced Mediterraneans; the other being the Irish gift for dalliance, typified in Dublin city where no matter how urgent his business, no Dubliner would pass a friend in the street without stopping to talk and maybe even taking time for a cup of coffee or a drink — or several. This has led to near-apoplexy on the part of an increasing number of foreign investors, but in time they get used to it, or else despair and simply go away.

Meanwhile, the eating and drinking and what can only be called 'con-viving' proceeds with vigour. The food is good, though like so many other recently-affluent people, the Irish are reluctant to serve traditional dishes like Irish Stew and Coddle outside their own homes. But there is plenty of magnificent fish — lobsters, oysters and salmon still cheaper than anywhere else in northern Europe — excellent meat, and marvellous, rough-textured brown bread.

Hotel and restaurant prices are high by British standards, but there is an encouraging increase in the quantity and quality of middle-priced establishments. At the upper end of the market *Ernie's Restaurant,* in the Mulberry Gardens at Donnybrook, and the *Lord Edward,* near Christ Church, are two of the best. In the middle range the restaurant in the National Gallery and *Mitchells* in the cellars of the famous wine merchants of the same name give excellent value, though the latter only opens for lunch. The attractive glass-roofed shopping centre in the courtyard of 18th-century Powerscourt Town House has plenty of cafés and restaurants, the best of them being *Timmermans* which is situated in the original kitchen of the house. Dublin has its share of Italian restaurants of various styles and standards, and one of the most popular with government officials and academics is the *Mini-Unicorn* in a little mews off Merrion Row. At the top of the pub-grub league is the Victorian *Stag's Head* which serves lunches and early dinners of substantial dimensions at an uncommonly reasonable IR£4.00. Like every other sizeable city in these islands, Dublin also has its greasy spoons, its burger joints and its pizza emporia, and these come into their own with the young, the indigent and the visitor whose holiday budget is exhausted.

County Dublin: North

West of the 1,800-acre Phoenix Park, which holds the residences of the President of Ireland, the Papal Nuncio, the American Ambassador and the Zoo, Dublin reaches out along the Liffey, by Chapelizod — named for that Kerry princess, Isolde, who gave such overwhelming inspiration to Wagner — to the wooded, suburban village of Lucan: Patrick Sarsfield held the Earldom of Lucan here before the Bingham family and enjoys a much better reputation with the Irish than the later incumbents. More interesting for the visitor, however, is the drive north along the shore of Dublin Bay, through uninspired suburban architecture — though a small diversion inland to Marino reveals one of the best examples of Palladian design in a lovely little Casino — past Clontarf, where King Brian Boru defeated the Danes in 1014 and lost his life on the same day, to Howth.

Howth

This rugged, heathery headland dominates the surrounding countryside with considerable grandeur, and on a clear day the view from its summit extends as far as the Mountains of Mourne in Northern Ireland. Beneath it on the north side shelters the little fishing village of Howth, which somehow manages to preserve its old-fashioned charm despite its proximity to Dublin (ten miles away), the presence of a smart restaurant, the *King Sitric,* and of the longer-standing Abbey Tavern where Irish ballads are sung.

Howth Castle, much altered since its foundations in the 12th century, is still in the hands of the family who built it, and the gardens are very popular with Dubliners in summer when a vast profusion of rhododendrons climbs a tall cliff. From Howth, too, boats go out to the little island known as 'Ireland's Eye', uninhabited now but with a 7th-century church to prove its importance in Early Christian times.

Portmarnock and Malahide

Further north along the coast are the small seaside resorts of Portmarnock, which has a championship golf course, and Malahide, where the same family has lived for some 800 years in various incarnations of the local castle. It was begun in the 12th century, and the three-storey tower house survives from that period. The slender towers flanking the façade are from the 18th century, while the interior of the house is notable for a Great Hall that still retains its mediaeval shape, and rich carving in the 16th-century oak room. It was in Malahide Castle that Boswell's diaries were discovered earlier this century, and today the house, which is open to the public, displays a portrait collection from the National Gallery and a fine exhibition of 18th-century Irish furniture. The gardens contain upwards of 5,000 different species and varieties of plants.

Inland Ruins

Rush and Skerries and a chain of other small seaside resorts stretch out along the coast north of Malahide, providing good beaches within easy driving distance of Dublin, while inland there is plenty of evidence of earlier civilisations. The oldest is represented by a cruciform passage grave with carved lintels and uprights at Fourknocks. There are a Round Tower and mediaeval castle remains at Swords, while the Round Tower at Lusk has spectacular company in much later circular towers at the corners of the neighbouring 16th-century building. Built on the site of an Early Christian anchorite cell, St. Doulagh's near Portmarnock claims to be the oldest church in Ireland and boasts a 12th-century stone-roofed chancel to prove it.

County Dublin: South

Chester Beatty Library

On the south side Dublin city runs quickly into the expensive suburb of Ballsbridge, where the Royal Dublin Society is the site of the fashionable Dublin Horse Show. There are several embassies in this area and, most important of all, the Chester Beatty Library with its great collection including superb Persian miniatures and early Egyptian papyri. The late Sir Chester was a man with diverse interests in many countries: an American naturalised in Britain, he made a fortune in mining in America and Africa and endowed Dublin, where he had a house, with the priceless legacy of this library.

Coast Road to Coliemore

From here on the road follows the coast most of the way to Dun Laoghaire, where cross-Channel boats come in and an imposing line of hotels rises above the harbour. It curves along the shoreline then, past private houses, out to Sandycove and the Martello Tower which Joyce shared with Oliver St John Gogarty, later immortalising both tower and friend in the opening of *Ulysses*. The tower is now a museum, so cosy and well heated that Joyce might never have left it had it been in that condition in 1904.

It is a short run then along a road which climbs and falls to Dalkey where a 16th-century tower is still planted firmly in the main street; and to Killiney Hill which gives a fine view of Dublin and the Liffey Valley. This is a justly fashionable residential neighbourhood with immediate access to the sea through the long beach at Killiney and through tiny harbours almost hidden from the road. Above Bullock Harbour there is a restored 12th-century castle, which is open to the public, and from Coliemore, it is possible to take a boat out to Dalkey Island which has the remains of an Early Christian church sacred to St Begnet.

Antiquities

Unfairly perhaps, the majority of visitors do not come to Dublin to tour the antiquities of the county. But there are plenty, some sign-posted, some not, ranging from megalithic tombs and dolmens of very early date through Early Christian and medieval remains. The best introduction to them is Peter Harbison's scholarly and exhaustive 'Guide to the National Monuments of Ireland' which includes illustrations, reference maps and such vital information as where to apply for the key. This should be consulted in conjunction with the same writer's more recent work on pre-Christian Ireland by all those with a serious interest in Irish antiquities.

Dublin Mountains

The Dublin Mountains stretch away to the east, with the ruins of the notorious Irish 'Hell Fire Club' more impressive from a distance than near at hand. Traffic permitting, it takes no more than half-an-hour's informed driving from the city centre out through the suburb of Rathfarnham, where a much-renovated 16th-century castle now houses a boys' school, to the mountains with their pine forests and glens and lakes; and for visitors travelling south, this is the most picturesque route of all into County Wicklow.

County Wicklow

Wicklow is a region of devastating beauty — assuming one has a taste for mountainous terrain, wild and inhospitable enough to impede the normal advances of urban civilisation. In many ways it forms a microcosm of the magnificent, desolate scenery that covers so much of the west of Ireland, but in Wicklow the reality is on a small and convenient scale, requiring hours, as against days, for the average traveller's cursory exploration. Weeks on end may easily be spent walking in the wooded glens or climbing amongst the mountains, but the instant tourist may cut the whole thing short, yet not short-change himself, by driving straight through the heart of the landscape, from the Dublin foothills to the borders of County Wexford, in about two hours.

Like every other county in Ireland, Wicklow has its share of antiquities but, except for the gentle ruins of Glendalough, most visitors pay more attention to scenery than to history in this area — and given the endless heaps of historic stones available for inspection throughout the rest of the country, they have some reason. Nature has had a helping hand from local residents, too, and County Wicklow holds more than its share of famous gardens which are open to the public. Some of them belong to historic stately homes which participate in the Festival of Music in Great Irish Houses in June.

History

For many years the granite, domed mountains of the region proved so intractable that Wicklow could hardly be brought within the jurisdiction of the Pale, less still secured for any length of time. Many a refugee held out there long after the rebellion in which he was involved had been crushed, or sometimes froze to death in the high, inhospitable moorlands; the outlawed O'Toole and O'Byrne families had martial innings lasting for decades amongst the mountains, from which they made savage forays against the forces of the Crown, and it was not until after the 1798 Insurrection, when it was decided that Wicklow must at last and somehow be brought under control, that the centre of the region was opened up with the building of the Military Road from Rathfarnham to Aughavannagh. Today it is the most popular scenic route through the county, giving access to the 'Featherbed', the Sally Gap, Glendalough and Glenmalure.

Wicklow Mountains

Even now, however, there are none too many roads through the wilder parts of Wicklow — which is all to the good. Those roads that exist are fairly narrow, though reasonably surfaced; ideal for leisurely touring, except at summer weekends when the whole of motorised Dublin seems to pour out across their own, neighbouring hills to picnic, practise their driving and generally clog up the little thoroughfares for miles. It is, after all, their country; but all the same, from the visitor's point of view, far better to explore Wicklow on a weekday when the nature-loving natives are more or less securely tethered to their jobs.

Then only the wandering sheep and the natural contours of the landscape impose caution, and do it very efficiently, too, while the eye travels for miles across sloping moors of heather and gorse; over deep, still, clear lakes and down steep valleys with rushing streams and what are surely the greenest forestlands in creation. Although it comprises a sizeable tract of country, Wicklow hardly seems big enough for the immense variety of scenery it contains: generally speaking, the steeper glens and more obviously spectacular scenery are on the eastern side, behind the flat coastal strip, while towards the west the mountains relax into broader, gentler valleys.

Two routes to Glendalough

Driving from Dublin the most attractive routes are out by the Military Road, through the Sally Gap, by deepset Luggala and its mansion, to Roundwood and Annamoe; or west from the city, by Blessington with its lakes through Hollywood to the Wicklow Gap.

From Roundwood, which has a nice little 17th century inn, it is possible to explore Lough Dan and Lough Tay; and at Annamoe local people still point out the spot where the youthful Laurence Sterne fell into the millrace: 'hundreds of people flocked to see me', confirms the novelist. From Hollywood on the other road it is a worthwhile excursion through the village of Donard to the natural amphitheatre of the Glen of Imaal. Here at Derrynamuck the cottage which sheltered the 1798 rebel, Michael Dwyer, has been restored in traditional style with rope chairs, settle bed, roasting spit and churn of the period.

Glendalough

Both these roads fetch up ultimately, as so many roads in Wicklow do, at Laragh, where the meeting of several glorious glens culminates in the peaceful climax of Glendalough. Steep, wooded slopes enclose the still lake waters, and along the shoreline are scattered the remains of one of Ireland's most celebrated monastic cities. It is the most romantic setting imaginable, and even now in its deserted solitude preserves a serenity which has no suggestion of the forlorn.

Glendalough was founded in the 6th century by St Kevin and over the years became a famous seat of learning which attracted students from most parts of the civilised world. Despite the offensive attentions of the Norsemen, it survived into the 14th century, and the ruins, evocative and beautiful in their silence, are extensive.

They include the ancient gateway to the city (approached by modern steps), several churches and a cathedral, the priest's house, the Deer Stone and St Kevin's Well, crosses, the foundations of a 'beehive' cell or *clochán,* near-perfect Round Tower, and St Kevin's Bed. Local legend has it that this last, which is a small man-made cave some 30 feet above the lake, is where the saint fled to avoid the temptation of a female demon bent on his corruption: she may perhaps have been an emissary from earlier deities associated with the ruined Bronze Age fort on the eastern shore of the Upper Lake.

Vale of Avoca
The Vale of Avoca, where the meeting of two rivers inspired one of Tom Moore's best-loved songs, lies south of Glendalough along a wonderful, wooded road. The tree beneath which the poet is believed to have browsed and composed and communed with nature is now dead, and its defunct remains protected from the greedy hands of souvenir-seekers by a railing. A mile or two away 'Avondale', which was the home of Charles Stewart Parnell, is now an attractive museum with a nature trail curving through the woods around it.

Mountain Village
Avoca makes a good base for exploring south County Wicklow, but inevitably it is heavily patronised by tourists, and better places to settle in peace and get the feeling of the countryside are Woodenbridge near the old gold mines where there is another meeting of waters; or Aughrim near the junction of yet two more rivers and only ten miles from Lugnaquilla, which at 3,039 feet is the highest mountain in the Wicklow range. Between them lies the desolate valley of Aughavannagh and, eastwards towards the Vale of Clara, Glenmalure where tradition identifies a series of stone walls as the former stronghold of one of the O'Byrne chieftains.

Wicklow Coast
Resorts and Gardens
Wicklow is fortunate in the unspoiled simplicity of its numerous small inland villages, whereas the bigger towns on the coast have profited by their situations to develop conventional seaside trade. Arklow in the south and in the north Bray, which has a magnificent headland, are the most popular; they are thronged with holiday-makers during the summer, but along the coast between the two are smaller, and

to many tastes more attractive, resorts such as Greystones and the county town of Wicklow. The latter has a ruined castle standing on a rocky promontory above the sea, the remains of a 13th-century Franciscan friary and, in an otherwise conventional 18th-century church, a fine Romanesque doorway from an earlier period. Less than ten miles south of the town the wide, smooth sands of Jack's Hole and Brittas Bay are popular for bathing and picnic parties.

There are famous gardens within the vicinity of both Bray and Greystones. There are striking works of art in the gardens of Dargle Glen, and a restaurant, too. At Kilruddery near Greystones the grounds present the only surviving 17th-century layout in Ireland, with twin canals, woodland theatre and fountains. Kilruddery House shows alterations carried out by Richard and William Morrison in 1820 and is one of the centres of the Festival of Music in Great Irish Houses.

Behind the Coast Road
The hand that ladled out the scenery neglected no part of Wicklow, and even the broad main road that sweeps south from Dublin to Wexford makes its way through lovely countryside with never more than a small turning off needed to take the traveller back into the mountains.

Behind Bray, for instance, within the shadow of the conical Sugarloaf Mountain the pretty village of Enniskerry sits in a wooded hollow and gives access to Powerscourt Demesne with its 400-foot waterfall and marvellous formal gardens. To the north on a direct route to Dublin lies the 'Scalp', a primeval rocky defile which provides a perfect example of the 'dry gap' sometimes formed at the end of the Ice Age; to the west lies the rugged valley of Glencree which shelters a German war cemetery.

Behind Ashford lies the Devil's Glen, a deep, rocky chasm, heavily overgrown, with the Vartry River rushing along its bed to plunge down to the basin of the Devil's 'Punch Bowl' almost 100 feet below in the rocks. Near here the Dunran Glen exhibits weird natural rock formations, while back beside the main road, at Ashford, stand the man-made beauty of Mount Usher Gardens. The home of the Walpole family who were Dublin's principal linen merchants for many decades, Mount Usher was laid out long enough ago for its luxuriant vegetation, some of it sub-tropical, to have come to maturity, and the gardens are open to the public.

A short run further to the south near Rathnew, *Hunter's Hotel,* which is one of the oldest coaching inns in Ireland, has very pretty gardens of its own and an irresistible atmosphere of quiet hospitality.

Western Wicklow
The landscape is blander in the western area of the county, and from

Leinster

Blessington Poulaphouca Reservoir stretches out, covering a considerable area and supplying water for the city of Dublin; the cataracts of Poulaphouca are a few miles south. Near here stands Russborough, a magnificent mansion in the Palladian style with splendid interior plasterwork. Now the home of Sir Alfred Beit, it houses the famous Beit art collection and also an outstanding collection of old Irish silver. The gardens are open to the public, and the house is another centre for the summer music festival in historic buildings.

Piper's Stones

The River Slaney rises in the Glan of Imaal, and near Hollywood, at Athgreany, the 'Piper's Stones', a circle of thirteen granite boulders derives its name from the bagpipe music said to be played there by the local fairies. The road continues in a wide south-easterly curve to Baltinglass which is just inside the Wicklow border in the Slaney Valley. The remains of the 12th-century Cistercian abbey here are said to belong to a foundation established by the same Leinster king, Dermot MacMurrough, who takes credit for inviting the Normans to Ireland. On Baltinglass Hill there are prehistoric passage graves and a fort.

County Wexford

Wexford is a golden, well-ordered county, its coastline swinging round to face both the Irish Sea and the Atlantic, its inland borders marked by the rounded contours of the Blackstairs Mountains in the west and the sterner profile of the Wicklow hills due north. The further south, the sandier the soil becomes until the small country lanes run past old Norman ruins half buried by the drifts of centuries.

History

Known variously as the 'Model County' or the 'Rebel County', depending on the mood of the moment, Wexford was the site of the Norman invasion which led to all the trouble in Ireland, and over the centuries its people erupted into violent hostility against the forces of the Crown. Their fiercest and proudest bid for freedom was the great rising of 1798, and there is hardly a village in the county without its memorial to the Roman Catholic priest, Father John Murphy, who led the insurgents, or else to the 'Croppy Boy' — a term deriving from the short-cropped hair-style then popular in revolutionary France. In fact, the '98 Rising was one of the few which had any degree of success: it spread rapidly through the county and into Wicklow, where it was well supported, but in the end the rebels, armed mainly with pikes and pitchforks, were forced back on Vinegar Hill, the small but striking eminence dominating the town of Enniscorthy, and there surrounded.

Long before the Normans came however, Wexford was a thriving

Norse settlement, and it is hardly too fanciful to trace this descent in the fair hair and ruddy complexion so common amongst the people today. They are unassuming, friendly folk now, diligent farmers and good neighbours who, despite their strong sense of history, live amicably with the many English families who have settled in the county: the same man who gives tongue to a '98 rebel ballad with as much feeling as if the whole thing had happened yesterday is likely to be dining with his English neighbour in easy friendship the same evening — which is surely a victory for civilisation.

South and West of Rosslare

Rosslare and Carnsore Point
For many visitors Ireland begins at Rosslare, where the British Rail car ferry comes in. Many of them get no further than the immensely long, sandy beach there and the championship golf course, the incongruous palm trees somehow surviving unmerciful whippings by the sea winds in winter, and the deep comfort of *Kelly's Hotel* which is known all over the country for its superb food and cultivated wine list.

Within easy reach of Rosslare is Carnsore Point, an unexpectedly rugged rocky outcrop pushing into a rich sea-fishing area, and in the village of Carne the *Lobster Pot* bases its menu on fish and shellfish fresh from each day's catch.

South of the Point Lady's Island stands in a sea-inlet and is connected with the mainland by a causeway. It holds the ruins of a Norman castle and priory of the 12th century, while not far away, at Tacumshane — where the 'father' of the American navy, Commodore John Barry, was born — there is a 19th-century windmill, restored in the 1950s but sadly not in use any more.

Kilmore and Clonmines
The road goes on, westwards, to Kilmore Quay, a little fishing village noted for its lobster catches and facing out towards the Saltee Islands. These form a sanctuary for millions of birds, including kittiwakes, guillemots and razorbills, but unless they are confident of calm weather boatmen are reluctant to take out visitors.

The coast turns north towards Bannow Bay where the Normans landed in 1169. The countryside is sandy here, suggesting that much evidence of the invasion may have been buried by drifts over the centuries, but at Clonmines, near the head of the bay, there are the impressive ruins of a mediaeval city. Clonmines received its charter early in the 13th century, but even before that it had been settled by the Norsemen and had its own mint; although it began to decline during the 17th century, it continued to send members to Parliament up till 1800. One of the old town gates, later turned into a kiln, still survives at

Clonmines, and there is a 15th-century tower, known as the Town Hall, the remains of two churches and fortifications from the same period. Drifting sand did as much as strife and politics to put an end to the prosperity of Clonmines, but although the old port probably became sanded up about 1600, some of the huge stones of the harbour wall are still visible. On the western side of the bay, Tintern Abbey, daughter house of the great Cistercian foundation in Wales, stands in picturesque ruins amongst trees in a quiet field, its fortifications long since abandoned. Cromwell is said to have slept here — but then, there is hardly a church in Ireland where he did not, apparently, quarter either troops or horses or both.

Hook Head to Dunbrody Abbey

The road south goes on through the village of Fethard, by Baginbun Head, where a joint force of Norse and Irish were defeated by the Normans, to Hook Head. Slade Castle here combines architecture of both the 15th and 17th centuries to handsome effect, while below the lighthouse on the Head the clear water attracts skin-divers, often as early in the year as April.

An attractive road runs from the Hook north along the western shore of Waterford Harbour to Duncannon, where a vast fort once guarded the waters of the estuary; to Ballyhack with its mediaeval castle remains, and on to the great monastic ruins of Dunbrody. Austere and lovely, Dunbrody with its nave and choir and transepts, plus some surviving domestic buildings, is one of the largest foundations in Ireland: the church, nearly 200 feet long and 140 feet wide at the transepts, still has a fine lancet east window with three lights, a richly decorated west door and rows of Early English arches separating the nave from the aisles. The picture of tranquillity and dignity it makes is piquantly at odds with its history of disputed possession amongst the clergy of the 14th century.

Kennedy Memorial

Dunganstown, where a great-grandfather of the American president, John Kennedy, was born, is further north along this road, and his cottage, much refurbished, may be inspected by visitors. In memory of the late president a fine arboretum has been planted on the slopes of Slieve Caollte.

New Ross

At the northern end the harbour waters become the estuary of the River Barrow and this leads upstream to New Ross — which with its narrow streets, its steps, its cobbles and its tall, old warehouses is one of the most attractive towns in the county. The River Nore joins the Barrow just above the town, and these gentle waters may be explored at ease by means of a cruising restaurant, moored at New Ross and providing first-class value in lunch, afternoon tea and dinner. The countryside around is utterly peaceful, with occasional houses rising from the green fields and sometimes woods dipping down to the water to create a strange tame-jungle effect above low mud banks.

Wexford Town

River Slaney
The Nore and the Barrow serve several counties, but from the time it crosses the border, the Slaney is Wexford's own river and makes its way in a great slow sweep south to emerge at Wexford Harbour. Just two miles outside the town of Wexford its broad rush-fringed expanse narrows suddenly to pass rapidly between the steep, wooded heights of Ferrycarrig with a fine 15th-century keep.

Below the keep there is the splendid *Ferrycarrig Hotel*, idyllically situated with an excellent conservatory restaurant facing grounds that slope down to the estuary. For less grand occasions, the *Oak Tavern* is only a few minutes away and gives good value in steaks and salmon and shellfish.

History
Wexford town was a place of consequence from time immemorial. It was marked on Ptolemy's map as 'Menapia' and under the Danes, from whom its present name derives, became a prosperous commercial centre. The Normans under Robert Fitzstephen took it a few days after their landing at Bannow in 1169, and from then on its history was frequently turbulent — the highlight being 1798 when the insurgents held the town for a month; the most tragic being the Cromwellian massacre which reduced the population by two-thirds.

Despite a splendid modern bridge swooping in from the north across the Slaney, the town retains a great deal of old-fashioned charm with its railway line running along the quay, and the narrow streets and lanes which reflect perhaps its earlier Norse design. Although the harbour has been blocked by a sandbar for many years now, its low stone walls still stand and Wexford's maritime background is recalled in a museum lightship moored at the quay.

Selskar Abbey; Bull Ring
Older memories than that are revived by Selskar Abbey where Henry II is said to have done penance for the murder of Thomas à Becket, and by a surviving fortified gate from the five that once pierced the town walls. Commodore John Barry has a lofty statue to his memory down at the harbour and in the centre of town is the Bull Ring where the sport of bull-baiting was practised by the local gentry; the focal point of the Ring is now the bronze figure of a '98 pikeman.

Opera Festival
A very active Old Wexford Society sees to it that the town and its buildings are well documented and there are excellent guided tours,

but Wexford might still be no more than a pleasant backwater were it not for the extraordinary phenomenon of the Wexford Opera Festival. This unlikely annual event takes place towards the end of October and, since its establishment more than thirty years ago by a local doctor of immense musical intelligence, has acquired an international prestige which attracts singers, critics and opera-lovers from all parts. Several guesthouses in the town cater for the overspill from the hotels, though for motorists the best choice is *Killiane Castle* about three miles outside Wexford. Here in a Victorian farmhouse adjoining a picturesque Norman keep, Mrs Kathleen Mernagh provides comfortable accommodation, good food and a welcome second to none.

The atmosphere in Wexford is remarkable during the festival, for although the principals may not have a word of English between them, and the operas are most likely to be the works which have not been heard in London, let alone Ireland, for over a hundred years, it is intrinsically the town's own creation and depends on the voluntary work of local people for its survival.

Shop assistants, farmers, landed gentry, businessmen: every man and woman in Wexford, plus a substantial number of children, seems to be involved in getting the opera on the stage; and townspeople who have never studied any foreign language will happily spend months learning choral parts in Italian, French, German and, when needs be, Russian. The austere little theatre holds less than 600 seats, and when the curtain comes down, often after midnight, audience and artists tend to mingle in the pubs, which have a special licence, and exercise their voices in less exalted music.

The restaurants and bars in the town's hotels stay open late, too, and there is much jolly partying to and fro between the *Talbot* at the southern end of the quays, and centrally-situated *White's*, which began as a coaching inn in the 18th century and has long been an integral part of local life.

Castles
There are two important castles within easy reach of Wexford: Johnstown is a 19th-century Gothic structure on the site of an earlier building, and is now an agricultural institute with fine gardens open to the public. Rathmacknee on the road south to Rosslare is a good example of classic 15th-century architecture.

Northern Wicklow
The Coast
Slightly north of Wexford the village of Curracloe is the nearest of a chain of small seaside resorts with big, sandy beaches extending all the way along the coast to the county border; Courtown, Ballymoney

and Cahore are the most popular of them and are within easy reach of the town of Gorey, where there is a splendid hotel and restaurant at *Markfield House*.

Inland: Enniscorthy

Going north from Wexford, Enniscorthy is the most picturesque inland town in the county. Spreading out along the banks of the Slaney, with Vinegar Hill in the background, the town grew up around the local castle, which was first established in the 13th century but re-built later in its present form. Although it remained a private dwelling until well into the present century, it is now a museum of engagingly unorthodox character. Relics of the 1798 Rising are housed side by side with old-fashioned farm implements, newspaper clippings from 1916 and a myriad collection of diverse objects which have more to do with real life than so many of the scholastically-documented exhibits of conventional museums. There is a strawberry fair in Enniscorthy in the summer, but for the rest of the year the little town is quiet enough, inviting leisurely inspection of its steep, hilly streets, its Pugin cathedral and the brief ascent of Vinegar Hill for a fine view of the surrounding countryside.

Ferns

The Blackstairs Mountains rise on the horizon in the west, and the best base for exploring these is the market town of Bunclody. In its day, however, by far the most important town in north County Wexford was Ferns. Today its pre-eminence is only a distant memory but it was here that the Leinster king, Dermot MacMurrough, retired, consolidated in this position by his Norman allies and, it is alleged, duly rotted alive. Certainly, the first abbey he built at Ferns was burned within two years, by accident or design, but the remains of a slightly later building survive in a church with a square tower rounded at the top. There are also ruins of a 13th-century abbey, while the present Church of Ireland building incorporates portions of the old cathedral; there are some plain High Crosses in the graveyard, and a fragment of a shaft said to mark the grave of the treacherous king. On high ground outside the present little village there are the remains of a 16th-century church, unaccountably furnished with a Romanesque window, while Ferns Castle, dating from the 13th century, is now in substantial ruins, its dignity sadly impaired by the latter-day addition of a concrete handball wall.

Counties Kilkenny and Carlow

Kilkenny City

Kilkenny and Carlow counties run into each other, and share pretty, undramatic scenery and a measure of colourful history. The city of Kilkenny was the seat of an independent Irish parliament about three centuries ago, and although today it functions basically as a market town, the survival of narrow, winding streets and of a number of important buildings illustrates its historic lineage and preserves a good deal of mediaeval atmosphere.

The city began, like so many others in Ireland, with an Early Christian monastic foundation, and the present St Canice's Cathedral, which dates principally from the 13th century, occupies the site of earlier churches. Much restored during the 19th century it retains most of its mediaeval distinction, houses a fine collection of tombstones of the 16th and 18th centuries and shows effective use of the local black marble. Beside it stands a Round Tower of earlier date.

But the city's secular standing began near the end of the 14th century when James Butler, third Earl of Ormonde, purchased Kilkenny Castle and went on to establish his family as one of the most powerful in Ireland. Its prestige was rivalled only by that of the two great FitzGerald families, the Kildares and Desmonds, and in time stricter allegiance to the Crown brought the Butlers out on top; they had meanwhile produced a wife for Sir William Boleyn, whose daughter, Anne, became Queen Elizabeth's mother.

Kilkenny Castle
Kilkenny Castle stands on high ground beside the River Nore, which flows through the city; despite inevitable alterations over the centuries, it still retains the lineaments of a massive mediaeval fortress. About a decade ago it became the property of the Irish Government and is now preserved as a national monument with the craft centre of Kilkenny Design Workshops housed in the former stables.

Other Major Buildings
It was in 1366 that the Statutes of Kilkenny, forbidding the Anglo-Normans to fraternise with the native Irish, were passed, but by 1642 the two cultures had merged sufficiently to allow the formation of the Confederation of Kilkenny and the parliament which represented the interests of both Irish and Norman stock for six splendid years. An influential dignitary of the period was Bishop Rothe whose house, built in 1594, has recently been restored and is now occupied by the Kilkenny Archaeological Society. Near it is the 14th-century home of Dame Alice Kyteler, a well-to-do local lady who, when accused of witchcraft, took off for England and left her maid, Petronilla, to be burnt at the stake. By 1693 Dame Alice's home had become an inn, and since its recent restoration has been in use as an eating-house.

Kilkenny's important churches, all of them dating originally from the 13th century, include St John's Priory, once known as the 'Lantern of Ireland' because of the multiplicity of windows in the Lady Chapel; the 'Black Friary' built by Dominicans, and the Franciscan 'Grey Friary' which is now accessible only through the local brewery. There is also a fine 18th-century *tholsel* or exchange, two almhouses, and in Kilkenny College the 18th-century successor to the school which numbered Swift, Congreve, Farquhar and Berkeley amongst its pupils. A few miles outside the city 15th-century Clara Castle still has its original oak floor-beams — and also a dungeon accessible from the privy on the fourth floor.

South Kilkenny

Thomastown to Inistiogue
South of Kilkenny city, Thomastown has the remains of a large 13th-century church, and at Ladyswell an enchanting little spectacle in a small roadside water garden, still powered by 19th-century pumps. The countryside around here is rich in mediaeval remains, and by far the most important is the vast ruin of Jerpoint Abbey. Irish-Romanesque chancel and transepts form the earliest part of the building, and there is a 15th-century square tower with the characteristic Irish stepped battlements. The ancient high altar from Jerpoint is now in the Catholic church of Thomastown.

There is a pre-Norman church, a Round Tower and a stone bearing inscriptions in *ogham* at Tullaherin, while from Thomastown a lovely road branches off for Inistiogue on the River Nore and beyond it the ancient church of Clonamery; then turns north to make its way back towards Kilkenny through Graiguenamanagh on the River Barrow.

Inistiogue
The countryside, green and wooded, dips gently down to the river which is spanned by a graceful ten-arched bridge at Inistiogue. Once an orderly compact tenant village of the Tighe family, Inistiogue has a tree-lined square, a sun dial, the ruins of a 13th-century priory, and an excellent restaurant called *The Maltings*.

A steep hill leads up out of the village to the shabby gateposts and rutted drive of Woodstock: this fine 18th-century home of the Tighes was burned in 1922, and its gaunt skeleton — blind windows staring inwards at the overgrown and utterly destroyed interior — is one of the most desolate and evocative ruins in Ireland.

Graiguenamanagh; Duiske Abbey
In the shadow of Brandon Hill, the village of Graiguenamanagh has a pretty situation on a bend of the Barrow river. The great Cistercian abbey of Duiske, which was established here at the beginning of the 13th-century, held a position of vast importance amongst Irish religious foundations until the suppression of the monasteries during the Reformation. The Earls of Ormond took possession of it then, though the monks remained in the area for many years, but in 1774 its tower collapsed and it was a ruin throughout much of the 18th-

century. In 1813 it was shoddily re-roofed to provide a parish church, and later in the same century there were crude attempts to restore the west. The more sophisticated techniques of our own time have superseded these makeshift efforts, and Duiske Abbey is now restored to something of its former glory with handsome arches and decorated capitals.

North-west, on the road back to Kilkenny, the 13th-century church at Gowran has several fine effigies from the period dating from the 14th to the 17th centuries.

Thomastown to Callan and Granagh Castle

Thomastown is also a good starting-point for visits to the mediaeval ruins of Kilfane church, which has a 13th-century effigy of a knight in full armour, and for Knocktopher where some of the remains of a priory founded by the earls of Ormonde in 1356 have been incorporated in a private house. Midway between Thomastown and the ancient market town of Callan lies Kells, once a formidable monastic settlement — though nothing to do with the monastery in Meath which produced the Book of Kells — and now a ruin of some substance with mediaeval churches, towers, domestic buildings and fortifying walls.

It stands within a walled enclosure, fortified by turrets and divided into two courts by a stream from the King's River and by a high stone wall with a central gateway. The church and monastic remains are in the northern courtyard, while the southern contains six dwelling towers, one adjoining the inner great door, four on the south curtain wall and the last forming the fortification of the priory's east gate.

Callan itself has ecclesiastical remains from the 15th century, and there are High Crosses further south at Killamery and Kilkeeran. Down near the county boundary with Waterford stand the ruins of Granagh Castle which overlook the river and were partially restored as recently as 1925.

North Kilkenny

Dunmore Cave

North of Kilkenny city the landscapes are sterner, and the immense Cave of Dunmore marks the site of a Viking massacre in which 1,000 people are said to have lost their lives. Known in ancient Irish literature as the place where the monster, Luchtigern was slain, the cave has yielded the bones of many victims thought to be the result of the Norse raid. It has several chambers, one of them holding a vast stalagmite known as the 'Market Cross'.

Castlecomer to Carlow

The main road north leads into hilly country to Castlecomer, which until recent times was the centre of Ireland's coal-mining industry. To the west lies the village of Freshford, neatly placed in a gap in the Slieveardagh Hills, where an 18th-century church retains a sculptured Romanesque doorway from an earlier building; further west and north are the ruins of a church and Round Tower at Fertagh, and at Ballyragget there are the remains of a large 15th-century Ormonde castle. The main road, however, runs east of these to cross the county boundary into Carlow.

County Carlow

The Blackstairs Mountains in the east, and the green, wooded landscapes formed by the two rivers that divide the county, make Carlow ideal for easy, leisurely touring. The Barrow and Slaney rivers are good for salmon and trout, and the former also offers an alternative means of touring. Entering Carlow above the county town it is navigable down as far as St. Mullin's, and is considered one of the loveliest inland waterways in Ireland. There is an active boat club in Carlow town, and cruising craft may be hired there.

Carlow Town
The county town of Carlow, which is the centre of the Irish sugar beet industry, was much embattled in the past. Its situation on the borders of the Pale meant that its possession was frequently contested, and there was hardly a decade up to 1650 when one side or the other, Irish or English, did not assault, besiege or burn it. Today the only reminder of this turbulent history is the ruin of a Norman Castle — which in fact owes much of its destruction to a 19th-century doctor who blew up parts of it to make room for a lunatic asylum. In 1798 Carlow was again the site of a battle: 640 of the insurgents were killed, and the great gravel pits where more than 400 of them were buried are now marked by a large Celtic Cross.

East of Carlow; Tullow
There is more ancient history a few miles outside the town in Browneshill Dolmen, which with its 100-ton capstone supported by three standing stones, is certainly one of the heaviest in Europe. Haroldstown Dolmen in the east of the county has two capstones resting on ten stones, and in this area also are the ruins of Clonmore Castle, a former bone of contention between the powerful Geraldine Earls of Kildare and the Butler Earls of Ormonde.

The principal town in east Carlow is Tullow which has attractive river scenery. There is an ancient fort within a few miles of the town, consisting of four stone ramparts, the outer one being about 1,000 feet in diameter. To the south lies Aghade where the prehistoric holed stone gives rise to many legends.

South of Carlow; St Mullins
South of Carlow town are the villages of Leighlinbridge and Old

Leighlin. The former has the ruins of the 'Black Castle' which guarded an important bridge across the Barrow; although there was a castle here in the 12th century, it was superseded first by a monastery and then by the present fortified tower which dates from the 16th century. At Old Leighlin the mingled styles of the 13th and 16th centuries may be discerned in the cathedral.

The awkwardly re-named village of Muine Bheag, formerly Bagenalstown, is within easy reach of the ruins of the castles of Ballyloughan and Ballymoon, the latter with its thick granite walls keeping notable fireplaces and doorways in good preservation.

In the extreme south of the county the ruins of St Mullins honour the memory of the 7th-century St Moling whose assiduous practice of politics resulted in tribute concessions between the provinces of Leinster and Munster. The present remains are mediaeval, but the 7th-century Book of Moling contains a plan of the original monastery.

County Laois

Portlaoise and Surroundings
The Slieve Bloom Mountains separate County Laois from Offaly in the north-west, and apart from some low, gentle hills to the south-east, the only other noticeable elevation in the county is the great Rock of Dunamase near Portlaoise. The surrounding countryside is flat, so that the 200-foot eminence assumes imposing proportions by contrast, and inevitably its summit is crowned by ruins.

Rock of Dunamase
It was in use as a fort in Early Christian times and belonged to King Dermot MacMurrough at the time of the Norman invasion. It passed through several hands during the centuries that followed, including those of the O'More family who had once been the ruling clan in the area and, though dispossessed of their lands at an early stage, continued battling against one aggressor after another for many decades. The fortifications were disarmed by the Cromwellians in the 17th century and, despite later efforts to restore it to residential standards, Dunamase fell into decay. Today the battered remnants of the old fortress are approached through the banks and ditches of its earliest defences, then through a bailey and outer gate, then a gateway with double turrets in a curtain wall. The inner court has a massive rectangular tower dating from the 13th century.

Portlaoise
The town of Portlaoise was an important strategic point in earlier times, and the site of many bloody conflicts. Only a single wall of its ancient fortifications still remains, and the most striking building today is the jail — from which some IRA prisoners made a dramatic escape

a few years back. Artefacts dating back to about 800 BC were discovered by a farmer quarrying sand on a ridge near the town some years ago.

Ballyfin
In the nearby village of Ballyfin the Patrician College is accommodated in a house designed by the Morrison brothers and believed to be the best of its kind in the country, while in the same area there is a splendid example of the work of the Irish Georgian Society in the restoration of Roundwood House, now a guest house. There is a Gibbsian doorway, a Venetian window and central breakfront, while the interior is remarkable for a staircase of Chinese Chippendale workmanship.

North of Portlaoise

Portarlington
A number of roads radiate from Portaloise, and eleven miles to the north lies Portarlington, which is the second-largest town in the county. It supported a Huguenot colony until comparatively recent times and has a 'French church', but the most prominent landmark in the vicinity is the cooling tower of the electricity station. This was the first peat-fired generating station in the country for, after the war, during which there was a severe shortage of fuel, Ireland began to turn its vast areas of bogland to practical account. Today this traditional fuel of the Irish poor is as widely used — highly processed, cheap and compact — in hydro-electric schemes and other industries as in the home. It has a distinctive and agreeable smell, best savoured on a winter's evening by an open fireside in a Connemara cottage.

Lea Castle
The ruins of Lea Castle are about two miles east of Portarlington. The town which once surrounded this old fortress was destroyed during the 14th century, and the castle itself changed hands several times before the Cromwellians captured it in 1650. Protected by a wall with inner walks, it is a square building with turrets at the corners; a window in the north face of the tower suggests that it was built about half-way through the 13th century.

Emo Court
In the vicinity of Portarlington stand 18th-century Emo Court and Coolbanagher Church, both the work of James Gandon, which marks the only time the celebrated architect was persuaded to exercise his skill in a rural area. The church is a simple, handsome building of immense dignity and contains an elaborately-carved stone baptismal font from mediaeval times. Emo Court is built in graceful neo-classical style and its fine gardens, which are open to the public, hold a wealth of splendid trees and shrubs and statuary.

Mountmellick to Montrath

Mountmellick at the northern end of the Slieve Bloom is a neat little village founded by Quakers and almost completely encircled by the Owenmass river which flows into the Barrow nearby. A road westwards leads from Mountmellick to the neighbourhood of Clonaslee where there is a fortified 17th-century house, and in the same area the castellated remains of 19th-century Brittas House. A particularly pretty road known as 'The Cut' travels back over the Slieve Bloom Mountains to Mountrath, which provides a good starting point for walking excursions into the mountains.

South of Portlaoise

Aghavoe; Heywood House

On the Tipperary border Borris-in-Ossory shows little sign of its former importance, but at Aghavoe there are some fine remains of mediaeval churches. Much of the decorative masonry however was removed to Heywood House near Ballinakill in the south of the county, and was damaged when the house caught fire some years ago. The Heywood estate is now the property of a religious order, which is supervising a youth scheme intended to restore the magnificent Italian gardens designed by Sir Edwin Lutyens at the beginning of this century.

Abbeyleix

At Abbeyleix the demense of the de Vesci family is open to the public. It is said to resemble a Black Sea estate laid out by a Russian ancestor of the De Vescis, but the house is pure 18th-century Wyatt: although not open to the public, its graceful outline may be seen from the grounds. Built late in the 18th century it is a handsome three-storey building with seven bay fronts and three bay pedimented breakfronts. This was O'More territory in ancient times, and a distinguished member of that family defeated the Earl of Essex at the 'Pass of the Plumes' in 1599. One of his forebears is recalled in an effigy dating from 1502 in the gardens of Abbeyleix, while the present pretty 18th-century village stands on the site of a monastery established by yet another early member of the same clan.

Ballaghmore; Durrow

Ballaghmore is Fitzpatrick country, and the castle here sports a *sheelagh-na-gig* (a lewd sculpture) facing derisively towards the traditional enemy in the neighbouring province of Munster. Cullahill, Gortnaclea, Kilbreedy and Aghmacart are all marked by the remains of the strongholds of former powerful clans, but at Durrow there is more recent and very beautiful architectural history in the local castle which was the first great Palladian house to be built in Ireland. It is now a convent.

East of Portlaoise

Stradbally

A pleasant road runs east from Portlaoise to Stradbally, where the steam traction museum attracts thousands of enthusiasts for its annual rally in August. This is the only time of year when the steam locomotive used by Guinness's during the last century is deployed on the narrow-gauge railway.

Timahoe; Killeshin

There is a stone hill fort at Clophook in the limestone hills south of Stradbally and megalithic remains in the area around Lugacurran and Boley Hill. Further south at Timahoe a comparatively late Round Tower has Romanesque decorations of heads with intertwined hair on its door. Similar decoration features in the capitals of the doorway which is all that survives of the Round Tower of Killeshin. There was a monastery there in the 5th century, but the present church ruins date from the twelfth.

Kildare and North Leinster

Northern Kildare

The world is full of people who could go straight to Kildare without realising that it is in Ireland. With the single-minded passion that distinguishes the racing fraternity, trainers, owners, punters — all are rapturously familiar, by name at least, with the great grassy sward of the Curragh which stretches from Kildare town north-east to Newbridge.

The Curragh; Punchestown

This is the heart of Ireland's horse country: animals bred at the National Stud have made their names all over the world, and Punchestown and the Curragh are two of the most important race-courses in the country.

Those whose visit coincides with a race meeting in Kildare might be forgiven for thinking that the county is wholly given over to the horse and its attendants. But at the eastern end of the Curragh, for instance, a deep hollow is named after a 19th-century boxing champion Dan Donnelly, and still bears his outsize footprints. The hero's arm is allegedly on display in a pub in the village of Kilcullen. North of the Punchestown course a nine-ton Bronze Age monolith rises nearly twenty feet above the ground. Even at Tully House the National Stud shares ground with elaborate Japanese gardens laid out to symbolise the vicissitudes of man's life.

Carton House; Castletown

Kildare is Geraldine country, the region most closely associated with the powerful Norman Fitzgerald family which came within measurable distance of threatening English sovereignty in Ireland and in the end was duly dismantled for its trouble. Inevitably there are remains of

Leinster

Geraldine strongholds all over the area (Nurney, Lackagh and the Lady Chapel of the ruined Grey Abbey at Kildare town), but the finest monument to their lost splendour is Carton House, once the home of the Dukes of Leinster, now a private residence and so kept up in style as it should be.

A few miles away, at Celbridge, Carton has a fitting architectural partner in Castletown. The building of Castletown began in 1722 for William Connolly who was then Speaker of the House of Commons. The impressive façade with its graceful, curving colonnades looks out over a fine two-mile view to the arched obelisk of Connolly's Folly, built for the Speaker's widow in 1740. Within the house the hall and staircase, with plasterwork by Francini, the Print Room, the Red Drawing Room and the ornate Long Gallery have all been painstakingly and expensively restored by the Irish Georgian Society, which now uses the house as its headquarters.

Robertstown; Grand Canal
The Irish have a talent for reviving their fine old buildings in this manner, at least for short spells, and at Robertstown, which is an attractive little backwater village on a junction of the Grand Canal, the old hotel and warehouses regain something of their former vivacity with the Grand Canal 'Festa' in August. The River Barrow connects with the Grand Canal and its waters moving gently through the pretty countryside of Kildare, Carlow and Kilkenny down almost to New Ross are now popular for cruising holidays. There is plenty of coarse fishing in the area, and pleasant walks along the tow path from Robertstown to the little 18th-century village of Prosperous.

Leixlip
Leixlip, further north on the county border with Dublin, has the benefit of a swift and turbulent stretch of the River Liffey which provides irresistible entertainment for canoeists. There is an active canoe club, which welcomes visitors, and a nice family-run hotel that gives good value in its 'Tourist Menu'. Leixlip Castle incorporates two mediaeval towers, one square and the other round.

Maynooth
But of all the regimes which have flourished and faded in County Kildare, the power represented by Maynooth, just west of Leixlip, is proving the sturdiest of them all — to date at least. Once exclusively the principal seminary in Ireland for the training of Roman Catholic diocesan clergy, Maynooth has now expanded to fulfill the function of a secular university as well. It was founded towards the end of the 18th-century, and over the years evolved around a Gothic-revival square inspired by Pugin to form a massive complex. The ruins of an early Fitzgerald castle stand nearby, and the juxtaposition provides a piquant illustration of the transient nature of power.

Southern Kildare

Kildare Town
While the grandeur of the 18th-century is superbly represented in County Kildare, there is plenty of evidence of earlier civilisations, too. The cathedral in Kildare town stands on the site of a monastery said to have been founded by St Brigid in 470 AD; the present building incorporates remnants from the 13th-century and has some mediaeval tombs. Nearby is a Round Tower of earlier date — one of the few which the public is allowed to climb: it has a fine Romanesque doorway, but the usual conical cap has been replaced by a stepped parapet.

Mediaeval Christian Remains
There are the remains of a 19th-century High Cross near the ruined Round Tower at Old Kilcullen, another High Cross and monastic remains at Moone Abbey, and at Castledermot in the south of the county an impressive concentration of mediaeval remains.

At least nine parliaments were held in the ancient fortress in the days when that institution followed the king's representative about the country, but there is more interest now in the mediaeval Christian site with its two granite High Crosses dating from the 10th-century and its handsome Romanesque doorway. One of the earliest High Crosses in the country may be seen a few miles north at the tiny village of Moone. Dating from the 8th-century, it is in a fine state of preservation and exhibits a wealth of intricate carving on its stone surface.

Athy; Kilkea Castle
In Athy a 16th-century Geraldine castle overlooks the river, and about six miles away is much-restored Kilkea Castle where, it is alleged, the eleventh Earl of Kildare practised magic. The castle is now a luxury hotel and to date no visitors have seen the 'Wizard Earl' who, it is said, from time to time follows traditional custom by exercising his silver-shod white horse in the Curragh.

Jigginstown; Rathcoffey Castle
Outside Naas, which is the administrative centre of the county, lie the immense ruins of Jigginstown, a palatial manor begun in 1636 by the Earl of Strafford as a possible residence for Charles I. Building however, was interrupted by the Earl's execution in London in 1641 and never completed. The ruins of Rathcoffey Castle to the north were once the home of the Chevalier Wogan, an adventurous Jacobite who joined the Irish Brigade on the Continent, rescued Clementina Sobieska at Innsbruck and escorted her to Bologna to wed the Old Pretender.

Dun Ailline
Long before the gallant escapades of Fitzgeralds, Wogans and

Wentworths, the ancient Kings of Leinster had a seat at Dun Ailline, where there are the remains of a massive hill fort, while the legendary Fionn Mac Cumhaill, commander of the heroic warriors of the *Fianna*, is believed to have resided on the summit of the Hill of Allen. It was a good place to choose, for the hill dominates the surrounding country-side and commands splendid views in all directions. There is a 19th-century folly at the top.

Louth and Meath

County Louth

The Valley of the Boyne attracted settlers from the very earliest times. The High Kings of Ireland lived at Tara, and together with the neigh-bouring county of Westmeath, the surrounding countryside was known as 'Royal Meath'. Other accounts suggest that Meath and Louth once formed a single kingdom and, judging by the immense quantity of prehistoric remains in the area, this may well have been so. The earliest are probably the court cairns at Aghnaskeagh, built, it is believed, by primitive farmers c. 3000 BC.

Coastal Villages

Today Louth is the smallest county in Ireland, despite a long coastline reaching from the Boyne through wide sandy beaches and occasional rocky headlands, northwards to Carlingford Lough and the moun-tainous scenery of the Cooley Peninsula. With populations numbered in hundreds rather than thousands, the villages of Greenore and Omeath form popular holiday resorts on the peninsula, while at Carlingford, beneath Slieve Foyle, the massive ruins of King John's Castle recall the formidable outposts of the Pale. There are ruins of a 14th-century Dominican abbey here, too; a square keep dating from the 16th-century and a towerhouse known as 'The Mint' from the same period, while a gateway of the old town walls is now part of the *tholsel* and forms an arch above the road.

All the way along the coastline to the south there are small seaside resorts and fishing villages — Blackrock, Annagassan, Clogher, Baltray — and behind them a second chain of inland villages, each with historic associations and ruins.

Cuchaulainn and Queen Maeve

A few miles away at Ratheddy stands the *Clochafaermore*, a landmark in Irish legend which recounts that when the hero, Cuchaulainn had at last been mortally wounded, he threw his sword into a nearby bog and tied himself to this stone so that he might die standing upright; his enemies remained at a distance until a raven came and perched on his shoulder and it was clear that he was dead. There is a small statue of the scene in the General Post Office in Dublin.

Many of Cuchulainn's feats were performed in wars with the male-volent Queen Maeve of Connacht, and right down into recorded history the provinces of Ulster, which were the homelands of Cuchulainn and the Red Branch knights, and Connacht sustained fierce antag-onism. But the most celebrated battle of all is retailed in the *Táin Bó Cuailgne* saga, an account of the Queen's illicit attempt to capture the Brown Bull of Cooley: her entire army was taken on one by one by Cuchulainn, who defended the ford, and the battle ended with the killing of the hero's childhood friend, Ferdia. Despite Cuchulainn's victory, however, Maeve got away with the Brown Bull.

Ardee
All this happened at Ardee, which clearly remained a place of impor-tance long after the mighty ones had become the stuff of legend. Its significance continued into the 18th-century as the surviving mace and sword and seal of the Corporation of the time confirm. These may been seen in the 13th-century castle on the river walk along the ford while, not far away, another castle built about two hundred years later is conveniently furnished with a 'murder hole' above the main doorway. Hatch's Castle, also a 15th-century building though equipped with Tudor windows, is now a private house.

Mellifont and Monasterboice
There are several castle ruins in the vicinity of the villages of Dromiskin, Dunleer and Termonfeckin, as well as monastic ruins dating from the 10th-century onwards. But by far the most impressive ecclesiastical remains are the great foundations of Mellifont and Monasterboice.

The most perfect High Cross in Ireland is at Monasterboice, while at Mellifont the great ruins of the first Cistercian abbey in the country spread out in tranquil, rural surroundings, its octagonal lavabo long since deprived of its central fountain, its tombs no longer revealing the names of their occupants — though Dervorgilla, who ran off with Dermot MacMurrough thus precipitating the Norman invasion, is said to be amongst them.

Dundalk; Ballymascanlon
Dundalk is the administrative capital of County Louth. Its original site to the west of the present town is marked by a sizeable Norman motte and bailey above an Early Christian souterrain. It is associated with Cuchulainn who was born at Dun Dealgan, where an 18th-century pirate was later to build his stronghold. But there is far more ancient history four miles away at Ballymascanlon in a huge neolithic Proleek dolmen with its 46-ton capstone. A wedge-shaped gallery grave nearby dates from the Bronze Age.

After early Norman times the town of Dundalk moved nearer the sea, towards flatter land which today supports an immense bird sanctuary. Most of the buildings in the town are of comparatively recent date, though a 15th-century tower is incorporated in the church of St Nicholas, and the most spectacular of them is the austere Greek-revival courthouse which was put up in 1820. It has a Doric portico and behind this the roof is carried towards the interior by a series of pillars which leave the enclosure open to the winds until the main stairway is approached.

Louth Village; Castleroche
The ancient village of Louth, from which the county takes its name, lies well south of Dundalk. It is a tiny place now, but its former importance as the place where St Patrick appointed his first bishop, St Mochta, is attested by a small, sturdy house with a pitched roof of stone, dating from the 10th-century and named after the episcopal saint. The house is remarkably well preserved, but the nearby 14th-century abbey is in ruins. In this region an old house built by the Plunkett family displays a mixture of architectural styles, from the 15th-century to the nineteenth, while at Castleroche the dramatic ruins of a 13th-century fortress dominate the landscape from their commanding position on a pinnacle of rock.

Drogheda
In the south of the county at the mouth of the Boyne, Drogheda retains impressive mediaeval remains, the most important being the barbican of St Lawrence's Gate which is a perfect specimen consisting of two drum towers and a connecting loopholed wall. There are scant remains of a 13th-century Augustinian abbey, and the Magdalene Steeple is believed to have been added to an earlier church in the 15th-century.

A goodly number of 18th-century buildings survive in Drogheda, amongst them St. Peter's Church, the former mayoralty, the old *tholsel* with its clock tower and the Millmount Barracks. Built to command the crossing of the River Boyne, the Millmount stands above the original motte which marked the foundation of the town and was itself raised above a neolithic passage grave. The Old Drogheda Society has converted part of this historic barracks into a local museum with an interesting collection that includes painted banners of the former trades guilds and a traditional leather-covered Boyne coracle.

Up to the middle of the 17th century Drogheda was considered one of the four principal cities of Ireland and had the right to issue its own currency, but the Cromwellian massacre destroyed the town's spirit as well as its population. It surrendered to William of Orange after the Battle of the Boyne and it was not until recent times that Drogheda revived to become the busy industrial centre it is today.

With such a bloody history behind it, it is surprising to find any early building of non-military nature surviving within the vicinity of

Drogheda. But only three or four miles away, on the north bank of the Boyne, stands the big house of Beaulieu built during the last quarter of the 17th century, wholly unfortified and still in perfect condition. Recalling the Dutch bourgeois style of the period, it is a fine building of red brick with a steep roof and tall chimneys.

County Meath

County Meath's seven-mile coastline consists almost entirely of sandy beaches with nice little holiday resorts including Bettystown and Laytown. Inland, however, Ireland's central limestone plain is broken occasionally by low hills which are of immense significance in the early history and legends of the country.

Tara

The Hill of Tara, however, is the most important ancient site and the outlines of the palaces of the High Kings who made it their home may still be traced. The Hill of Ward was associated with a great *aonach,* or fair, held every three years at the Celtic feast of *Samhain* — which corresponds to November 1st in our calendar — in honour of the sacred fire lighted by the god, Lug. Its Iron Age ring-fort was badly damaged by fortifications put up during the 17th century, but there are still earthworks to be seen. The hill at Teltown was the site of the Tailteann games, named for the legendary Queen Tailte and again sacred to the god, Lug. They were celebrated at the beginning of August, which is called *Lughnasa* in the Irish language.

Tumuli

The Stone of Destiny still stands at Tara — whatever the current owners of the Stone of Scone may think — but the most spectacular pre-Christian remains are represented by the great tumuli of Dowth, Knowth and Newgrange just north of Tara. The decorated Boyne Valley tombs nearby are amongst the most impressive in the Western world, and two of them have now been excavated while archaeologists are still working on the third. Newgrange, once covered with brilliant white quartz, is about forty feet high and a long narrow passage leads beneath the mound to a great central chamber with corbelled vaulting narrowing to the climax of a single capstone. Dowth has two prehistoric tombs, one of them reached by climbing down a ladder and scrambling, sometimes crawling, along the entrance passage: it is worth the effort.

Prehistoric remains

All this part of the country holds prehistoric remains. There is an important Bronze Age passage-grave beneath a grassy mound at Fourknocks, south of Drogheda, while away to the west of the county, near the little market town of Oldcastle, the Loughcrew Hills are the site of some thirty chambered cairns; late Iron Age relics were uncovered here, and also a rich hoard of Bronze Age remains. The tomb on the central hill is richly decorated with a full complement of passage-grave motifs — spirals, circles, diamonds, chevrons, ferns and stylised suns.

Slane; Tara's Decline
All domestic trace of the builders of these vast cemeteries had vanished by the time the monarchy of Tara reached its peak; and although it remained a kingly seat until early in the 11th century, Tara itself declined with the coming of Christianity. But the importance of hill sites continued, and legend has it that St. Patrick chose the hill above the village of Slane for the lighting of the first Pascal Fire. Certainly there is evidence of an Early Christian monastery in the vicinity, but the building of this is attributed to St. Erc (sic) who was one of St. Patrick's converts. There are more tangible remains of the 15th and 16th centuries and, dominating the pretty little village with its four handsome Georgian houses, a fine castle designed by Wyatt in 1786. Although it was already in decline, the symbolism of Tara was still powerful enough for the last of the Irish High Kings, Rory O'Conor, to invoke it as a political gesture. He also held a final session of the Tailteann Games in 1168, all this within a decade of the coming Norman invasion which was to sweep away the lingering vestiges of native royalty.

Kells
One of the finest Round Towers in Ireland rises 100 feet at Donaghmore beside a ruined 15th-century church. At Bective Abbey near Navan, dark grey stone ruins recall a Cistercian foundation of the 12th century, while at Duleek remains date from the 10th century on into the seventeenth. More important than these, however, is the Early Christian foundation of Kells with its Round Tower, High Crosses and thick stone walls sloping inwards to form the roof ridge of 'St Colmcille's House'. Generally considered the world's finest example of the art of illumination, the Book of Kells was produced here in the 8th century; it is now on display in the Library of Trinity College, Dublin.

Trim Castle
The arrival of the Normans meant the construction of those castles and fortresses at which they excelled but, strangely enough, most of the castle ruins in County Meath — Athlumney, Dunmore, Dunmoe — date from the 15th century, and Robertstown Castle from the seventeenth. The glorious exception is Trim.

Situated on the south bank of the Boyne, the vast edifice of Trim Castle, its walls eleven feet thick, was completed about 1220. It was an invincible bastion of Norman power in the area, and towards the end of the 14th century the future Henry V of England was imprisoned there, with the Duke of Gloucester, by Richard II. Even today the ruins of the castle are a monument of formidable strength and grandeur, while on a ridge opposite, the shattered tower — known as the 'Yellow Steeple' — of an old Augustinian abbey is a reminder that Church and State marched hand in hand in times gone by. Nearby are the remains of a gate in the vanished town walls and behind St. Patrick's Cathedral the ruins of a mediaeval chancel reveal fine 15th-century windows.

Newtown Trim
Less than a mile downstream stand the ruins of the 12th-century foundation of Newtown Trim, built by the first Norman bishop of Meath in the Gothic style and in its day the largest cathedral in Ireland. The neighbouring mediaeval ruin was a hospital in which the *Fratres Cruciferi,* or 'Crutched Friars', nursed wounded crusaders.

Swift Mausoleum; Dunsany Castle
More recent history is recalled at Castlerickard by the Swift Mausoleum. The great Dean was the incumbent at Laracor from 1699 to 1714, and though his church and rectory have gone, the walls of the cottage where Esther Johnson, his beloved 'Stella', lived are still standing. The ruins of Dangan Castle in the same district are a reminder of the Duke of Wellington who was a boy there and had his early schooling at Trim, while near the village of Dunshaughlin stand the fine stone church and castle of Dunsany. The Dunsany family still lives there, and amongst the private collection of fine art and ceramics and furniture housed in the castle are a pair of paintings by Van Dyck which were presented to the Lord Dunsany of the time by Charles II in 1660.

Navan
Situated at the confluence of the Boyne and Blackwater rivers, Navan is the principal town of County Meath. Although it is Norman in origin and has a motte and uncommonly high bailey, only a fragment of a wall and a tower survive from the Middle Ages, and today the town is a thriving business centre deriving most of its support from local carpet and furniture industries.

Bunratty Castle, Co. Clare

Munster

Munster is like the sound of its name — big and strong and full of the noise and spectacle of surging seas. The two eastern counties, Tipperary and Waterford, are prosperous and agricultural and scenically much tamer than the south-west where the Atlantic forces its way inland in long, deep bays beneath tumultuous mountains. To the north lies the lush, rolling countryside of Limerick and above that, on the other side of the Shannon, County Clare with its strange and diverse mixture of scenery. To explore this region properly a car is essential, and it is worth setting aside plenty of time to do it thoroughly.

County Cork

Cork City

Cork is the largest county in Ireland, and Cork city the proudest and liveliest — less sophisticated than Dublin, less urban in character, but with an animated and individualistic charm that brooks no resistance. Corkonians are proud of their city, of their own ready wit and of their reputation for hospitality; and indeed, it would be difficult to spend a few days in the city without falling amongst friends, ruddy-faced and curly-haired, with distinctive accents and a picturesque turn of speech that owes much to the Irish language.

Cork is a well-to-do city and its people have an infectious zest for enjoyment, thinking nothing of driving sixty miles to a hunt ball and arriving back in time for a quick breakfast before the next day's work; or of sailing all day in frequently turbulent waters, then spending the night at a spontaneous party in the yacht club. The women tend to be elegant and well-groomed, the men with the prevailing thick jet curls, much given to checked sports jackets and cavalry twill. The same faces appear above more formal clothes during the annual Cork Film Festival in June, and themselves assume formal expressions in keeping with the dignity of the International Choral and Folk Dance Festival that takes place towards the end of April.

Almost impossible not to get lost in Cork at first. The city reaches out in every direction from an island in the River Lee, and what with bridges, one-way systems and dense traffic often geared to the pace of a horse and cart nonchalantly embedded in its motorised midst, the sharpest sense of direction is easily confused. A splendid road sweeps in from the north, past Blackwater Castle on the Lee; and the smart traveller will follow this to a car park, assume sensible shoes and then set out on foot — for happily, Cork is a city of manageable proportions.

Patrick Street
The centre is Patrick Street with its fine bridge facing the near-perpendicular slope of Patrick's Hill, and affording a view across the river to the red roofs of a housing estate known locally as the 'Kremlin'. Narrow streets and lanes lead off temptingly from Patrick Street, but the most practical course is to follow the wide, curving thoroughfare to its head: to the right lies Cornmarket Street and the Coal Quay where the sharp soft song of the Cork tongue plies rapidly in high-speed bargaining; to the left Grand Parade marches with dignity down to the pleasant broad reaches of the Mall where the quays begin.

The Quays
Bristling with shipping and industry, they are the most immediately picturesque facet of the city's life, for by and large Cork has few important buildings earlier than the 19th century, though there are a few 18th-century churches and plenty of domestic architecture from the same period. But essentially it is the haphazard design and lively atmosphere that give Cork its character — the twisting lanes, the sudden flights of steps linking old streets on different levels, the

staircases giving direct access from waterways to front doors.

City Centre

In recent years much work and money have gone into refurbishing the city, revealing the decorative details of its fine old buildings to advantage. The covered 'English Market' in the city centre is a picturesque and vivacious hive of trade, while in the vicinity of Shandon, the old Butter Market is being restored and transformed into a modern arts centre. This is on the north side of the Lee near the Church of St. Anne, where for a small fee visitors may try their skill at ringing the famous bells.

Hotels; Restaurants

There are plenty of hotels in Cork, some smart and svelte in the modern manner, others old-fashioned and quaint with distinctive personalities which will amuse or irritate according to individual temperament. Restaurants vary, but one of the best in Ireland is at the Arbutus Lodge Hotel where the cooking is seriously and successfully calculated to provide first-class international food, plus such local specialities as *drisheen,* a blood sausage which is served with tansey sauce. Another Cork hotel famous for its cooking is Ballymaloe House a few miles east of the city at Shanagarry.

Fine food apart, a visit to the *Oyster,* hidden in an alleyway off Patrick Street, is obligatory for anyone hoping to lay a finger on the pulse of local life. Wood panelling and plain cooking are the order of the day, and in the course of an evening the life of the city emerges most entertainingly in the racy anecdotes and repartee ricochetting around the bar — where immense quantities of excellent 'Paddy' whiskey are consumed.

Blarney

The village of Blarney is only five miles from Cork city. Its 15th-century castle is worth quite as much attention as the famous Stone, though the latter receives far more from thousands of tourists eager to contort their bodies leaning backwards into the castle machicolation to kiss it. The observance of this uncomfortable ritual — which must pose problems of hygiene for the fastidious — is said to confer the gift of 'blarney', a word deriving from Elizabethan times when the local lord prevaricated so assiduously in the matter of surrendering his castle that the Monarch declared his speeches were 'all Blarney; he never means to do what he says.'

Eastern Cork

The Blackwater river flowing east through the county takes in the pleasant north Cork towns of Mallow and Fermoy, but for visitors the coast is likely to prove more interesting. The eastern strip spreading out from Cork Harbour is dominated by Cobh with its vast

Gothic Revival cathedral and its landing station for passengers disembarking from the great Atlantic liners.

Fota Island
One of the principal attractions of the area is Fota Island where a splendid Regency manor, housing an important collection of Irish landscape paintings, is the centrepiece of a spacious wildlife park and arboretum. The house, which is open to the public, has some of the finest neo-classical interiors in Ireland and is decorated and furnished to match the style.

Ladysbridge to Youghal
It is an easy drive from Fota, via the pleasant market town of Midleton, to Ladysbridge, where there are the massive remains of a 17th-century fortified house, and on to Cloyne. Here, beside the ruins of a mediaeval cathedral, one of the famous Round Towers of the early Irish Church may be climbed for a panoramic view of the surrounding countryside, while amongst more recent monuments is the alabaster tomb of the 18th-century philosopher bishop, George Berkeley. Down on the coast the road to the east winds along the shore to Ballycotton Bay, past Garryvoe with its long, sandy beach, to round Knockadoon Head and enter Youghal where the Blackwater river flows between lush, wooded banks to join the sea.

Youghal
Youghal has been an important town since mediaeval times. Walter Raleigh was once its mayor, and it is said that he planted the first Irish potato there — an honour claimed in other parts of the country as well, though Youghal presses home its claim with the Walter Raleigh Gourmet Potato Festival every summer. The stately Elizabethan house where Raleigh lived is in reasonable repair, and it is believed that the poet, Spenser — who lived in the north of the county at Kilcolman Castle — often visited Raleigh in Youghal and wrote at least part of the 'Faerie Queene' in the house.

St. Mary's Church at Youghal dates from the 13th century but has been disfigured by rebuilding since then; an interesting feature remains, however, in pottery vessels placed behind holes in the chancel walls, apparently to improve acoustic conditions. A substantial portion of the old, fortified town walls still stands behind the church and includes two turrets. The Clock Gate dates from the 18th century, and there are two 16th-century buildings — one a former castle is now a grain store, and the other a deserted alms-house. Its own antiquities apart, Youghal is also a good base for exploring the ruins of Rinncru, Templemichael Castle and, in the neighbouring county of Waterford, Molana Abbey.

Western Cork
West Cork is a different world. It would take weeks to work thoroughly

in and out of the harbours, and harbours-within-harbours, that break up the coastline, growing progressively deeper and wilder as they travel westwards to culminate in the great inlets and peninsulas of Roaring Water Bay, Dunmanus and Bantry. The roads are bewildering in their twisting and turning and frequently sub-motorway surfacing, and it is easier, faster and smoother to take one of the main roads out of Cork city and branch off later for the coast — easier by far, but less rewarding. For those determined on rapid passage, Bandon is the main town on the road south to the coast, Macroom on the upper route going north-west to Killarney.

Kinsale

Those taking the coast road should not miss Kinsale. Only eighteen miles south of Cork, it is an unusually distinctive village with handsome slate-fronted Georgian houses rising on hills above the estuary of the Bandon river. Discreet face-lifting has not damaged its old-world character, and here and there amongst the narrow streets the voluminous folds of the traditional Kinsale cloak, once worn generally by local women, may still be seen — though on close inspection the wearer is just as likely to be a smart Dubliner on holiday, her cloak a high-fashion replica of the original.

Kinsale Harbour is guarded by two magnificent 'star' fortresses of the 17th century, while to the north of the town a signposted trail marks the course of the historic Battle of Kinsale fought in 1601-2 between Spanish and Irish forces against the English. In recent years Kinsale has been developed with uncommon tact as a sea-fishing and gourmet resort, and local restaurateurs and hoteliers have shown exemplary enterprise by combining to buy wine in bulk in an attempt to keep prices at a reasonable level. Meanwhile, discreet modernisation enables the establishments where the precious stuff is sold to merge without aggression with historic buildings like the early 18th-century Court House and 13th-century St. Multose's, which is one of the few mediaeval churches still in use in Ireland.

There is good bathing at nearby Summer Cove and Oyster Haven, and a fine walk to be made from the village past an old ring fort to the cliff scenery and castle ruins at the Old Head of Kinsale. It was off the Old Head that the *Lusitania* sank in 1915, and salvage work continues every summer.

Coastal Villages

Working westwards along the coast, the road goes through Clonakilty, and through pretty little seaside resorts such as Courtmacsherry, Rosscarbery and, prettiest of all, the villages of Glandore and Union Hall facing each other in woodland scenery across a tiny harbour. Small roads branch off and meander down to Castletownshend and Baltimore; and from Baltimore boats go out to the island communities of Sherkin and Cape Clear. These are all small, unassuming places now, but monastic remains on both of the islands suggest importance in the past, while on the mainland ruined castles recall the ruling families of Townshend and O'Donovan.

Beyond Skibbereen the mountains take over in earnest, forming gaunt backbones for the western peninsulas of the county. They are divided by Dunmanus Bay and Bantry Bay, the latter polluted by oil in recent years, and though the roads make few concessions to motorway standards the area is worth exploring for the sake of lovely, desolate scenery, sudden beaches, and cheerful little villages like Ballydehob and Schull and Crookhaven; Kilcrohane and Ahakista and Durrus. The landscape is wild, the roads often precipitous, the headlands of Mizen and Sheep so spectacular that the vast sandy crescent of Barley Cove comes as soft sybaritic relief.

Caha Mountains; Beara Peninsula
The Caha Mountains divide the Beara Peininsula between Cork and Kerry, and from Adrigole on the south side the road climbs steeply upwards to cross the ridge at the Healy Pass. But the peninsular road goes on down the coast, between mountains and sea, past the austere slopes of Hungry Hill, to Castletownbere. Offshore the long, narrow landstrip of Bere Island guards the harbour and a few miles outside the town stands the vast, roofless castle of Dunboy where the Irish chieftain, O'Sullivan Bere, held out for Philip of Spain until 1602. The road continues south, with a turning off for the former copper village of Allihies on the other side of the peninsula, then runs further out into the Atlantic until it reaches land's end where a cable car swings the brave out over the boiling waters of a rocky sound to Dursey Island.

Bantry Bay
Unlike its neighbours the headwaters of Bantry Bay are broad and tranquil, and the road which runs beside them from Bantry to Glengarriff is an easy, pleasant drive, with mountains in the background and in the foreground the ruined fortifications of the O'Sullivan Bere family on Whiddy Island. Twice in the past French fleets have sailed into Bantry Bay, first in 1689 in support of James II's attempt to regain the throne; again in 1796, with Wolfe Tone on board, to help the United Irishmen.

The waters of the bay come right up to the immense square which is the core of Bantry, and just beside the town stands Bantry House, built in 1750 with a south front added in 1840, the whole combining to present one of the most gracious Georgian mansions in Ireland. The house, which is open to the public, contains a priceless collection of tapestries and furniture brought from all over Europe to form an irresistible cross-section of history, while the gardens, designed with terraces and statues in the Italian style, command an unrivalled view of Bantry Bay.

Munster

Glengarriff; Garinish Island

From Bantry, past Ballylickey — where there is a fine guest house with excellent French cuisine — the road curves along the head of the bay to Glengarriff. This extraordinary lush little place, totally at odds with the stern peninsula to the south, stands at the head of a deep, secluded inlet, sheltered by mountains behind and providing fertile soil for an abundance of Mediterranean flora. Garinish Island, where Shaw is believed to have written his 'St Joan', lies in the mouth of the little harbour. Its Italian gardens blaze with colour in the summer and local fishermen take out visitors by the brimming boatful, for it must be admitted that Glengarriff is a very popular tourist centre, but fortunately the straggling nature of the village beyond its small centre helps to dissipate the oppressive effect of large concentrations of trippers and sightseers.

Mountain routes: Macroom; Mallow

From Ballylickey on the Bantry/Glengarriff road the motorist may turn off into the mountains to Kealkill. The road divides here to go by a circular route through the Cousane Gap to Dunmanway and back to Bantry; or north-east through the Shehy Mountains by Ballingeary and Inchigeela to Marcoom. There is an ancient castle here, many times damaged and rebuilt but now derelict and roofless. The Cork road goes on through the Boggeragh Mountains, bending east by the Blackwater river to run into Mallow. This former spa, which gave rise to the song about the notorious Rakes of Mallow, is a thriving market town, with a half-timbered Clock House, an old castle and of course, the spa well.

From Mallow it is possible to return to Cork city via Fermoy, which has a lovely situation on the Blackwater, or continue north, by Buttevant — which has monastic ruins and marks the turning-off for Doneraile and the ruins of Spenser's castle — to Charleville. There are the ruins of former strongholds of the Roche family in the vicinity and, about seven miles away at Kilavullen, the house, situated on a cliff overhanging the river, where the ancestors of the Hennessy brandy family lived.

Pass of Keimaneigh; Gougana Barra

By far the most popular routes, however, are those winding up through the mountains from Snave Bridge and Glengarriff to file through the Pass of Keimaneigh with its dramatic overhanging crags, which legend says was formed by the leap of a hunted deer from one side to the other. On the other side lies Gougane Barra, the source of the River Lee and a holy place from centuries back when Cork's patron, St Finbarr, founded a hermitage on the island in the lake.

Surrounded by the steep rock faces of mountains, often streaked by waterfalls, Gougana Barra has an impressive atmosphere. The lake is reached by causeway, and although St Finbarr's foundation has long since vanished, there is a chapel in his honour on the site, and the island is still a place of pilgrimage. Mercifully, neither fame nor devotion have spoiled it.

County Kerry

The People
In many ways a law unto itself, County Kerry (or the 'Kingdom of Kerry' as it is often called), is people by a race who seem to bear no relation to their neighbours in County Cork, less still to any other group in Ireland. They say that when murder is committed in the 'Kingdom', everybody knows who did it but nobody ever tells. Fortunately, such grim incidents are rare almost to the point of non-existence, and the tourist is unlikely to be molested.

In fact, Kerry people are generous and warm-hearted and gregarious; fiercely independent, highly individualistic and outrageously funny in their humour and cynicism and wit. Their use of words — articulated in a musical, singing accent — is elaborate and brilliant, the courtesy voluble and gracious, while behind it all there is a level-headed detachment that assesses the world without sentimentality. Characters to a man, every one of them, they have folk traditions so strong and vivid that, although the evidence of long-standing Christianity is profuse, a happy suspicion of ancient paganism survives, smiling beneath it.

The Countryside
Like the country flag, the colours of the countryside are green and gold, and the scenery of the two great peninsulas which form the climax of the whole south-western landscape, is breathtaking. It is mountainous of course, the most mountainous of the entire region, with the highest peaks in Ireland rising like a thunderclap above Killarney and dominating the lives of the people as they do the famous lakes beneath them.

But a high mountain in Ireland is hardly high by European standards: Carrantuohill, the highest of all, is only 3,414 feet. What Irish mountains have instead, and Kerry mountains in particular, is a formidable presence which obliterates consciousness of scale, a frequently malevolent grandeur that is only matched by the bare crags and slopes high above the meadows and forests of the Alps.

Long-distance walking routes, divided in approximate ten-mile stretches, total about 150 miles between the two peninsulas, while activity and adventure centres take full advantage of natural amenities. But its magnificent scenery remains the county's greatest glory, and is described in authoritative detail by the Kerry booklet, which is one of the best in the county-by-county series.

Munster

Kenmare; Beara Peninsula
The best approach to the adventure of Kerry is up through the mountains above Glengarriff in County Cork, through the dark, impressive tunnel of Turner's Rock beneath which the first panorama of the 'Kingdom' spreads out in a rare landscape of mellow farmland. Those travelling by the direct route via Macroom from Cork may turn off into a secondary road to drive through the romantic scenery of Glenflesk, a glorious valley showing striking evidence of glacial action long ago. Set well back from the roadside, a handsome old farmhouse called the *Salmon Leap* provides a perfect base for exploring this splendid hinterland, before travelling on by Kilgarvan down to Kenmare.

Kenmare Estuary
Situated at the head of a vast estuary, Kenmare is an attractive little town which reflects the orderly inspiration of an 18th-century landlord. A much earlier civilisation is recalled however by a local pre-historic stone circle with a recumbent burial boulder at the centre. Thanks to the vagaries of the Gulf Stream, seafood in this part of the world includes the prickly sea-urchin more commonly associated with the Mediterranean, and this unlikely delicacy is much in demand at the Park Hotel which is noted throughout Europe for its food.

Tuosist
Technically, County Kerry begins on the north-western side of the Beara Peninsula, but unaccountably the lovely and impoverished countryside north of the Caha Mountains, only ten miles south of Kenmare, tends to be neglected: is hardly known even to anyone beyond the immediate vicinity.

Its name is Tuosist, a scattered collection of small, poor parishes which have their administrative centre at the crossroads of Lauragh with stony mountain slopes rising in the background, and some of the loveliest lakes in the country at Clonee: easy to believe old tales of giants — perhaps akin to the trolls of Norway — striding down from the mountains to bury treasure in the lakes, where it lies still protected by the ancient wisdom of the fish. No one has yet succeeded in devising the magic formula which will persuade the fishy guardians to part with the treasure; no one even knows the nature of the buried hoard, but legend insists that it is beyond price and beauty and even wisdom itself.

There are no hotels in Tuosist, but visitors are happy to rent custom-built, self-catering cottages and villas in the neighbourhood, or to put up by the harbour in O'Sullivan's pub which specialises in seafood and enjoys an enviable reputation for the strength and savour of its mussel soup.

Lauragh
There is another good pub called the *Síbín* in the forest landscape of

Lauragh. This has belonged to the same family for 400 years, and though it is non-residential, offers a friendly welcome to those minded to wander in the lovely, undeveloped non-touristic country. There is often traditional Irish entertainment at the *Síbín* during the long summer evenings, while during the day there is plenty of leisurely diversion to be had in fishing and sailing, and in exploring the glorious woodland gardens of Derreen House. These are remarkable for the profusion and variety of their rhododendrons and azaleas which flourish alongside camellias, bamboos and New Zealand tree ferns.

Iveragh Peninsula

Ring of Kerry: South

Across the bay the Ring of Kerry is perhaps rather too widely cele-brated — which makes it none the less worth seeing, for the scenery of the Iveragh Peninsula is very fine and deserves thorough explora-tion, inland as well as along the coastal ring road.

From Kenmare as far as the Blackwater river which flows down from the mountains the road has few pretensions beyond castle ruins and the view across the water to the mountains on the other side. At Parknasilla, however, there is a sudden resurgence of lush, dense vegetation and the road curves inland to Sneem, then back down towards the coast through pretty, romantic scenery. At Castlecove there is a turning-off for Staigue Fort, an impressive prehistoric fortress standing isolated in a rocky amphitheatre amongst the mountains: the circular wall, which is up to eighteen feet high in places, is thirteen feet thick, and the interior is reached by a long passage covered with slabs.

Down on the coast, the Ring road goes on to Caherdaniel, and to peaceful, sandy Derrynane where the house of Ireland's 'Liberator' and architect of Catholic Emancipation, Daniel O'Connell, is set in the close shelter of wooded parkland; the house is now a museum. There are soft, sandy beaches here, and at low tide it is possible to walk out to the ruined church of Abbey Island.

The road rises some 700 feet now to the Pass of Coomakista, then winds gently down to Waterville, which is a lively summer resort with a big sandy beach between mountains and sea. A minor road wanders off from Waterville around the foot of the peninsula to the Irish-speaking farming communities of Ballinskelligs, and to Port-magee, which is connected now by bridge with Valentia Island.

Valentia Island; Skelligs

Site of the first transatlantic cable station, Valentia is a pretty island with woods alternating with fine cliff scenery and deep-sea angling waters which are held to be amongst the best in Europe. From here, and from points on the mainland, boats go out on a fine day to the

Munster

Skelligs, the three sharp rock pinnacles which rise dramatically from turbulent waters far offshore. On Skellig Michael, which rises 700 feet above the sea, a group of monks built a monastery about 1,000 years ago. The stone steps cut painfully into the steep rock are still there, as well as half-a-dozen drystone cells, round on the outside and square within; two stone oratories, a church and, most affecting of all, the echo of a small garden on terraces above the cliffs.

Ring of Kerry: North

Back on the mainland the Ring of Kerry continues on to Cahirciveen, an engaging little town where the best of the pubs is kept by a local poetess-cum-playwright, and from there the road works its cliff-hanging way along the northern coast of the peninsula to Glenbeigh. This tiny village has become one of the most popular places in Ireland, largely due to excellent food, fishing, riding and shooting facilities. Undoubtedly the best time to be in Glenbeigh, however, is the August Bank Holiday, when every man, woman, child, tractor, carthorse and donkey for miles around converges on the narrow road to Rossbeigh Strand for the annual races.

Puck Fair

The Ring becomes less spectacular on the way to Killorglin, an unspectacular place in itself — except for three hectic days in August when ancient paganism triumphs in the coronation of a goat as king of Puck Fair. It has been suggested that the honouring of the goat derives from an occasion when a stampede of a herd gave warning of an English attack, but it seems more likely that the custom goes back to pre-Christian ritual: whatever the origins, the town celebrates in a manner which the older deities would heartily approve.

Iveragh Interior

It is a short, easy drive from Killorglin to Killarney, but behind there is still the interior of the Iveragh Peninsula which handsomely repays an extra day's touring. The best way of tackling it is from Waterville up through a gaunt pass from which the descent in recollection seems to have been of the order of one-in-two. The road pushes on through a vast, empty green plateau, ringed by mountains, to lonely Glencar where the threatening spectacle of the Macgillycuddy Reeks challenges eager climbers. At Glencar the road divides, going left back down by Caragh river and its lake to Glenbeigh or, more impressively, left through the Ballaghbeama Gap, which is perhaps the most sinister pass in Ireland, and out on the coast again at the mouth of the Black-water river. It turns left again then for Kenmare and another short, but much more spectacular route via Moll's Gap to Killarney.

Killarney

The Lakes

Killarney is all that poets, tourists and anyone who has ever seen the place say it is, and the first sight of the famous lakes occurs on the Kenmare road at the vantage point of 'Ladies' View'. The road winds down beside the lakes, through rocks and trees, to Muckross, then through the town of Killarney and on to Aghadoe, which gives a fine view looking towards the Gap of Dunloe.

The lakes and their environs may be explored by boat, motor or jaunting car, or by a judicious blend of all three — for at Kate Kearney's Cottage, although not legally obliged to do so, tourists are rather forcibly expected to abandon motorised transport and hire ponies, although there is of course nothing to prevent them making the four-mile journey through the Gap on foot. Massive rocks crowd the narrow defile, which was formed by glacial action, and a turbulent stream drains small lakes along the way. The head of the Dunloe Gap is nearly 800 feet above sea level, and beneath it lies the Upper Lake of Killarney with the fastness of Black Valley stretching away into the mountains on the right.

The wooded shores and islands of the Upper Lake have a special charm, and from here it is customary to make the return journey to Killarney by boat, leaving the lake by a narrow channel which leads into a strait beneath the crags of the 'Eagle's Nest'. Great echoes leap back from the rocks, and red deer wander at will on the shore and through the woods.

Here boatmen ship their oars to shoot the rapids leading down past Dinis Island to the Middle Lake also called Lough Leane, where limestone caves are associated with the *Colleen Bawn* — although the murdered lady who inspired the famous story lived and met her death in the neighbouring county of Limerick. The Lower Lake is the largest of the three and on a fine evening its calm expanse reflects the outlines of the mountains towering above. There are about thirty islands on this lake, each one with at least one legend to its name, and the boat trip usually ends at Ross Castle, a 15th-century fortress which remained invincible until 1652 when the Cromwellian forces brought flat-bottom boats overland for its bombardment — thus ful-filling the prophecy that Ross might 'all assault disdain/Till strange ships sail upon Lough Leane.'

Muckross
Just outside Killarney town Muckross National Park provides acres of fine grounds for walking, with easy routes to Torc Waterfall and to the splendid ruins of Muckross Abbey which combines Norman and Romanesque architecture with later Gothic; Muckross House is a Victorian structure built in the Tudor style. All around the summits of the Reeks reach up into the skies; Carrantuohill, Purple Mountain, Torc Mountain and Mangerton are the most popular with climbers.

Killarney Town
With all this on its doorstep, it is inevitable that despite the dignity

of its Pugin cathedral, Killarney should be pre-eminently a tourist town — 'Tourist trap', visitors were wont to complain in times gone by, but matters have improved significantly in recent years.

To be sure, every second shop appears to be dedicated to the diverse products of the souvenir industry. But for the most part the shops are smartly painted and decorated, and their contents of reasonable quality and largely authentic. There are plenty of hotels of course, some outside the town in private grounds, others like the *Three Lakes* providing first-class accommodation, friendly service and ample parking facilities in the centre. The restaurant attached to the hotel makes a special feature of such traditional Irish dishes as bacon-and-cabbage and Irish Stew, while throughout the town a wide variety of restaurants specialises in local fish and seafood. At £10.00 per table d'hote three-course meal — which includes a welcoming cocktail on the house — *Sheila's* in the High street offers some of the best value for miles around.

Dingle Peninsula

South Coast
The last of the great Kerry peninsulas is Dingie, which lacks the ameliorating softness of Iveragh but has far more grandeur and dignity. From Castlemaine to the north of Killorglin, it reaches thirty miles out into the Atlantic, and the manner in which the whole landscape slides backwards, gathering itself for the final forward leap to Slea Head is unforgettably dramatic. A last, frantic attempt by the mainland to recapture the Blasket Islands, it seems, and all the more unexpected after the gentle, contented road leading out to Inch — where a long, golden tongue of sand leans out almost to touch Rossbeigh on the other side of the bay.

This part of Kerry is rich in history and pre-history, and at Fahan there are standing stones, ring forts, souterrains and over 400 *clocháns* — the circular, mortarless stone dwellings known locally as 'beehive' huts. Not all of them are pre-Christian, however, for the technique of this construction survived until the last century, and quite a few were built as outhouses in comparatively recent times. Inevitably, the epic hero, Fionn Mac Cumhail, features in legend here, notably in his gory three-day battle at Ventry to repel the invasion of the 'King of the World'. He was successful of course; and the encounter is described in detail in a 15th-century manuscript now in the Bodleian Library at Oxford.

The little port of Dingle is the principal town of the peninsula, and it is beyond here that the country becomes really wild and bleak. Past Ventry and Fahan a side route leads down to a dangerously-situated prehistoric cliff fort, while the coast road goes on to Dunquin, now reckoned to be the last parish before America.

Blasket Islands
The Blasket Islands, forlorn and lovely across the water, have been
abandoned this twenty years and more, but in their day they harboured
sturdy fishing and farming communities and produced three remarkable writers — Peg Sayers, Thomas O'Crohan and Maurice O'Sullivan
— whose Irish-language books are regarded as classics and are
published in English translation.

Boats make day-trips to the Blaskets in summer, and on the Great
Blasket deserted farmsteads may still be inspected as well as church
ruins. The smaller islands of Inishtooskert and Inishvickillane have
crosses and 'beehive' huts.

North Coast
There are great and small beaches on the peninsula coast in this
area, and northwards the community of Ballyferriter looks towards
Smerwick Harbour and *Dun an Óir,* the 'Fort of Gold', crowning a
rocky promontory above the site of the massacre of some 600 Spanish
and Irish soldiers in 1580. Near here, at Kilmakeddar, there is a
remarkable Hiberno-Romanesque church; a few miles away is the
perfectly-preserved drystone Early Christian oratory of Gallarus, while
between Ballyferriter and Ballydavid geologists are still puzzling over
the inexplicable intrusion of the flagstone, sandstone and shales which
are collectively known as the 'Dingle Beds'. East of Ballydavid Head,
Mount Brandon rises steeply, and most travellers retrace the route to
Dingle to cross the peninsula by the Connor Pass.

The ascent from the coast is gentle enough and flattens out briefly
on the summit to give fine views of Tralee and Brandon Bays in the
north, of Dingle Bay behind. The valley beneath has several lakes,
including one shaped like an Irish harp, and then the mood of the
mountain changes as the road edges downwards along the base of
great cliffs which overhang a wilderness of boulders.

Castlegregory
The unassuming rural charm of Castlegregory down on the shore
comes as welcome contrast after this, and it is startling to learn
that it is named after a family of violent propensity. Gregory Hoare
built the original castle, which has now vanished, and it was his son,
Hugh, who chose to entertain Lord Grey on the latter's way to deal
with the Spanish/Irish force at Smerwick. Edmund Spenser and Sir
Walter Raleigh were guests on the occasion, and acute was the
embarrassment when it was discovered that the intensely-patriotic
Mrs Hoare had expressed her resentment at the presence of the enemy
in her home by pouring all the wine in the house over the cellar
floor. The enraged husband promptly attacked and killed her, then
conveniently dropped dead himself before he could be arraigned for
murder. Lord Grey worked off his chagrin at Smerwick.

The flat sands of the Magharees and their little islands with Early Christian remains make a relaxing excursion before completing the tour of Dingle at Tralee.

Tralee

The chief town of the county, Tralee, is probably best known as the inspiration of the song written there by William Mulchinock, and an annual 'Rose of Tralee' Festival sees to it that his Mary is not forgotten. As the town was destroyed late in the 17th century, most of the older buildings, which include an impressive courthouse, date from the 18th and 19th centuries, though some mediaeval sculpture is incorporated in St John's Church.

Local initiative is now at work on the restoration of a 19th-century windmill, which will house a museum and traditional crafts, and on the revival of the old steam train service to Fenit in the north of the county. It is also hoped to get at least a section of the old single-gauge railway that once connected Tralee with Dingle in working order again.

Ratass Church; Ardfert Cathedral

Ratass Church is probably the oldest building in the vicinity. In the 12th century it was for a while the seat of a bishopric, and it was during this period that a chancel was added to the original 10th century foundation. Although the church is now in ruins, there are interesting artefacts in the shape of a broken pillar bearing a Greek cross and in an ancient stone commemorating a worthy of the 8th century in the primitive Irish calligraphy that is believed to have evolved on the Dingle Peninsula around the beginning of the Christian era.

There is another *ogham* stone near the imposing ruins of 13th-century Ardfert Cathedral a few miles to the north, and west of this more recent history is recalled by an earthen fort named for Sir Roger Casement who was captured there after his submarine landing at Banna Strand in 1916.

North Kerry

Coast Road

By contrast with the peninsulas, north Kerry is less exciting, but at Fenit there is a geological curiosity in a vast boulder resting on limestone at the edge of the water and, further on, a natural cave with many ramifications. The coast road runs out along Ballyheigue Bay, where there is a striking ruined castle, to Kerry Head. There is good cliff scenery here, and deposits of the clear and purple quartz crystals known as 'Kerry diamonds'. Beyond lies the big seaside resort of Ballybunion, with its great cliffs and sea caves.

Listowel

Inland, the market town of Listowel on the River Feale is dominated by the ruins of a 15th-century castle in the main square. Several well-known Irish writers came from Listowel, and every summer the town's literary heritage is honoured by a gathering of writers as eloquent in the spoken word as in the written. A three-day race meeting held in September galvanises the remainder of the population and a good part of the country as well.

Tarbert, Tarbert Island
There are remains of several ancient castles in this region, and at Tarbert, near the Limerick border, a splendid example of Irish Georgian architecture. In its spacious entrance hall, Tarbert House still has original gunracks and trestles, and its wealth of Georgian furniture includes a superb Irish Chippendale mirror. A ferry service to Killimer shortens the journey across the mouth of the Shannon, and from the village of Tarbert a causeway runs out to Tarbert Island with its lighthouse and ancient battery.

Limerick and Clare

County Limerick
The counties of Clare and Limerick spread out on either side of the wide Shannon estuary — the one poor in material resources but rich in strange, brooding scenery; in the other prosperous, with great green pasture lands, magnificent hunting and a strong place in Irish history. In a country so poignant with ruins, this region is exceptional in the number of historic castles which have roofs, are still put to good use and occasionally even lived in by descendants of the original builders.

Knights of Glin
The Knights of Glin, descendants of the Desmond Geraldines, have lived in the same place now for about 700 years, and the family's ancient castle, destroyed in 1600 after a fierce defence which culminated in hand-to-hand fighting on the battlements, stands near the present residence — a handsome manor set in a fine demesne reaching down to the banks of the Shannon on the Limerick side.

O'Briens of Thomond
The O'Briens of Thomond have also survived the vicissitudes of the centuries, and the present Lord Inchiquin can claim descent from the High King who broke the power of the Danes in Ireland. This was at the Battle of Clontarf in 1014, but while his power was still limited to Munster, Brian Boru had already taken Limerick from the Danes and it was a prosperous, peaceful port when the Normans arrived towards the end of the 12th century. Even these invaders were repelled, though only for a time, and in 1180 Donal Mor O'Brien began building St Mary's Cathedral. Only fragments from this period, including a Romanesque doorway, survive in the present building, which has been much re-worked: the magnificently-carved black oak choir stalls

date from late in the 15th century and the church bells from the seventeenth. Donal Mor's grave is in the chancel, and there is a fine monument to the Great Earl of Thomond, who died in 1624, in the north transept.

Limerick Castle
In 1210 King John visited Limerick and ordered a strong fortress to be built on the banks of the Shannon. This castle still dominates its surroundings, and despite damage and desertion, remains an impressive example of mediaeval architecture. In its time it played a prominent part in Limerick's defences, including the occasions when the city was in Irish hands — for after the Battle of the Boyne the defeated Jacobite forces withdrew to Limerick under the command of the Earl of Lucan who was then Patrick Sarsfield. William III besieged the city without success, but a year later a second Williamite army was victorious. The defenders, however, were allowed to march out with full honours, and more than 10,000 of them emigrated to France to join the armies of Louise XIV.

Treaty of Limerick
The Treaty of Limerick guaranteeing religious freedom for Roman Catholics was later repudiated by the English parliament, from which incident Limerick became known as 'The City of the Violated Treaty' — and lest anyone forget, the stone on which it is believed Sarsfield and the Williamite commander signed their agreement still stands on a plinth near Thomond Bridge.

'The Lily of Killarney'
It was in Limerick, too, that John Scanlon of Ballycahane House near Croom was tried in 1819 for the murder of his young wife, Ellen Hanly. This notorious and unsavoury affair inspired Gerald Griffin, a young newspaper reporter who was covering the trial, to transfer the events to Killarney and write a novel called the *The Collegians* — which in turn formed the basis of Boucicault's play, *The Colleen Bawn* and Benedict's opera, *The Lily of Killarney*. It is gratifying to know that although Scanlon was defended by the 'Liberator', Daniel O'Connell, he was found guilty and hanged.

Limerick City
In mediaeval times Limerick was divided into the 'English' town and the 'Irish', and the outlines of the rather haphazard planning of that period are still evident in the old quarter of the city, especially in the street around the fortified 15th-century house, called 'Fanning's Castle', where the mayor, Dominic Fanning, was living during the second siege of Limerick.

The 18th century, however, takes over in the busy neighbourhood of O'Connell Street, a wide shopping thoroughfare which leads un-expectedly into a quiet and lovely double crescent of Georgian houses.

In the city centre a fine Georgian warehouse has been restored and now houses the local tourist information office with attendant shopping and restaurant facilities.

Trade Centre
The great River Shannon, plus a canal link with Dublin, made Limerick for a time one of the busiest trade centres in the United Kingdom, and in the local museum there is a pedestal called the 'Nail' which used to stand in the old exchange and on which, according to tradition, merchants discharged their debts. It must be admitted that the city of Bristol across the Channel also claims to be the source of the expression, 'paying on the nail'. One of the most prestigious sources of its prosperity was the lace industry, and Limerick Lace is still made, though in much smaller quantity, by nuns in a local convent.

West of Limerick City
Although the remains of the 12th-century church are incorporated in the city Liberties, more tangible evidence of Limerick's history is scattered about the county, much of it inevitably within easy reach of the gentle south bank of the great estuary. West of the city at Mungret are the remains of two ancient churches, while at Askeaton lie the remains of the 15th-century Franciscan friary, and a much-embattled castle with a splendid dining hall. Towards the end of its useful days this last became the seat of a rather respectable version of Dublin's 'Hell Fire Club'. Near Shanagolden stands the 13th-century abbey which was once a nunnery: it has a pigeon-house and also a room called the 'Black Hag's Cell' where, legend says, the last abbess practised witchcraft, no doubt precipitating the downfall of the abbey thereby. A little further inland the thick walls of 13th-century Shanid Castle recalls the Desmond family who used 'Shanid Abu!' as their war cry.

South-west to Adare
The main Kerry road runs out from Limerick through the pretty little village of Adare. A model of neatness with its trim, thatched roofs, it was built by the Earls of Dunraven whose estates adjoin it. Adare Manor is a Gothic Revival building, but the demesne, which is open to the public, contains the ruins of a fine castle and two churches, one of them in the middle of the golf course. In the village two ancient monastic foundations are still in use, one as a school, the other as the parish church. The latter in fact consists of the tower, nave and choir of a ruined mediaeval abbey restored by the first Earl of Dunraven early in the 19th century.

Palatine Country; Ardagh
Below Adare the road runs into 'Palatine' country, so called for Lutheran refugees from the Rhine who were settled in and around Rathkeale at the beginning of the 18th century to serve as models of industriousness and devoutness to the intractable Irish. The

immigrants preserved their own customs and continued to speak German for about a century, but thereafter gradually became absorbed into the native population. The countryside here is rich in mediaeval remains, and Newcastle West is built around a large 15th-century Desmond castle with a well-preserved banqueting hall, now used for concerts and exhibitions. Earlier times are recalled by the ring-fort of Ardagh where real treasure was discovered in the 19th century. The most important piece is the Ardagh Chalice, a richly decorated, two-handled cup dating from about the 18th century; together with jewellery and a bronze cup, it is now in the National Museum in Dublin.

Lough Gur
Towards the east County Limerick runs into the fertile plain known as the Golden Vale, and appropriately Aine, an ancient Munster goddess of abundance, resided here near the town of Hospital. She had, apparently, a son by one of the Desmond earls and when he died his remains were taken to Lough Gur, which he has since haunted. His partiality for the place is understandable, for there are two old Desmond castles beside the horseshoe-shaped lake, and along the shores interesting megalithic remains. These include forts, stone circles, wedge-shaped gallery grave and neolithic housing sites, while in the lake an artificial island is evidence of a very early *crannóg,* or lake-dwelling.

South to the Ballyhoura Hills
South Limerick faces the Ballyhoura Hills which are an extended arm of the Galtee Mountains in Tipperary. Kilmallock, which is the principal town in this area, was founded by the now extinct White Knights of the Desmond family and was one of the most splendid towns in Ireland in its time. It still retains a gate from the mediaeval town walls, but the castle, the 15th-century Collegiate church and the lovely 13th-century Dominican friary have been in ruins for many years. Moving towards the hills Kilfinnane recalls another Palatine settlement, and in the valley of Glenosheen lies the former estate of Silver Oliver who encouraged the Rhenish immigrants to move south from Rathkeale. It was at Castle Oliver, they say, that Lola Montez — dancer, adventuress and celebrated mistress of Ludwig I — was born plain Marie Gilbert in 1818.

County Clare

Although it belongs in the province of Munster, psychologically and geographically Clare has more in common with the traditional West of Ireland — poor land, thinly populated and desolately beautiful in many parts. The famine hit hard here, and the countryside remained severely depressed until some thirty years ago when the enterprising Shannon Free Airport Development Company was set up to redress the situation through the administration of immense tax concessions for industry in the airport region, through the development of tourist attractions second to none in the entire country, and through the encouragement of indigenous crafts in remoter areas. It has been a remarkable success story, and today County Clare enjoys a degree of prosperity unknown in previous history. The people are amongst the kindliest and friendliest in Ireland, and take great pride in traditional music which flourishes in several specialist schools in the county.

The Burren

The eastern section is green and well watered by several lakes, there are fine seaside resorts along the coast, but it is the grim magnificence of the strange limestone area in the north-west that is the county's most unforgettable feature. Hard to believe that life ever managed to gain a foothold in the sinister landscape of the Burren: an unrelieved grey desert marches from a high plateau down to the Atlantic making no concession to prettiness, although the incongruous presence of low stone walls indicates that this wilderness is of concern to someone.

Pollnagollum and Aillwee Caves

Although it is very poorly populated today, the Burren in fact attracted enough prehistoric settlers for numerous tombs, dolmens and gallery graves to remain scattered about its inhospitable wastes; and in the Pollnagollum cave complex reaching seven miles into the mountain-side the bones of Arctic lemming, African wild cat, reindeer and elk were found, along with skeletons of wolves and bears.

There are two entrances to the complex, but exploration is not recommended to any but thoroughly experienced and well-equipped pot-holers. In the same region however Aillwee Cave, with its massive, prize-winning stone access hall, is open to the public and provides a fascinating tour of the infrastructure that supports the stern, stone mountains. Not to be missed.

Botanical Burren

While the Burren continues to tempt archaeologists from all over the world — as recently as 1934 a group from Harvard uncovered the remains of eighteen people with Bronze Age artifacts in a pre-historic cist grave — it holds equal if seemingly paradoxical interest for botanists. For despite its forbidding, rocky aspect, the shallow soil of the area nurtures an incredible profusion of flowers of different species. Mediterraneans co-habit incongruously with arctic-alpines, and every year the second half of May brings an invasion of eager botanists to look for roses, gentian, geraniums and the pretty little Irish orchid.

It would take weeks to exhaust the resources of the Burren, but the motorist may form a quick impression of the terrain in half a day by taking the Corkscrew Road from Lisdoonvarna to Ballyvaughan and returning along the coast by Black Head. There is a fine view of the Aran Islands, which are the last outcrop of the Burren, from here, and on the roadside a fanciful little pinnacled well-house where the water is always sweet.

The Admiral's Rest
Those with the time to spare for proper exploration can hardly do better than put up at *The Admiral's Rest* which stands above the fine beach and sandy dunes of Fanore in the shadow of Black Head. The simple cottage-style restaurant specialises in seafood from the local reefs, and its proprietor, a retired and genial sailor whose passion is the wild life and flora of the region, likes nothing better than the opportunity to conduct interested visitors about the countryside, pointing out such extraordinary phenomena as the white gentian which recently poked its head up amongst its vivid brethren, or the cave near 15th-century Ballynalackan castle which is believed to contain the longest stalactite in Europe.

Corofin; Kilfenora; Killinaboy
Below the Burren the landscape is softened by the numerous lakes in the vicinity of Corofin, and a traumatic period of Irish history is documented in the Clare Heritage Centre, which is situated in this agreeable little market village. An impressive collection of descriptive material about the geology, scenery, flora and fauna of the burren has been assembled in a display centre at Kilfenora, a village which used to call the Pope its bishop. There is a 13th-century cathedral here with three carved High Crosses in the churchyard, while at Killinaboy the mediaeval church incorporates the rare and lewd small sculpture known as a *sheela-na-gig*.

Leamanagh Castle
A few miles away one of the most dramatic ruins in Ireland rises starkly beside the road in the shape of Leamanagh Castle; the gates were removed to the plushier environs of Dromoland Castle during the last century, but the gaunt skeleton of the castle, built partly in the 15th century, partly in the 17th, remains tremendously impressive — even before its story is told.

This was an O'Brien stronghold and a cause of dissention between rival claimants in the family. In the mid-17th century its current incumbent Conor O'Brien went out to do battle with the Cromwellians and was mortally wounded. He was brought back to the castle where his wife, *Maire Rua* or 'Red Mary', thinking him already dead refused him admittance, declaring that she would have no dead men in the house she hoped to defend. On realising her mistake, it is said that she relented and nursed him until he died the same night; certain it is that the following day the redoubtable widow marched to Limerick to marry a Cromwellian officer and so keep control of her house and lands. Later she despatched this second consort by pushing him out of a top-floor window.

Lisdoonvarna
This sort of tale goes well in the shadow of the Burren, but a different and very jolly atmosphere prevails down at Lisdoonvarna which is Ireland's spa, noted for the efficacy if not the deliciousness of its sulphur springs. It is also a popular holiday resort and during the peak season in September unmarried local farmers gather there to relax after the harvest and, it is alleged, keep a weather-eye open for potential wives. Girls have been known to come from as far away as Dublin on the strength of this story, and recent years have seen the establishment of a match-making festival, no less!

Cliffs of Moher
South of Lisdoonvarna the road swings out to the coast and the famous Cliffs of Moher. These great promontories pushing out into the Atlantic extend south for about five miles and rise almost 700 feet at their northern end, where the land view is drearily defaced by a 19th-century tower put up by yet another scion of the O'Briens. Some amends have been made by the cliff walk laid out by the same gentleman. Hag's Head marks the southern extremity of the Cliffs and then the land curves east in the mouth of Liscannor Bay.

Liscannor and Ennistymon
John Holland, the inventor of the submarine, was born in the little fishing village of Liscannor, and the road south runs through this to Lahinch which is a big seaside resort with a wide, sandy beach. Inland the town of Ennistymon derives great charm from the wide, low falls of the Cullenagh river running through it, and great distinction amongst Irish literati as the birthplace of the 18th-century poet, Brian Merriman. His masterpiece, 'The Midnight Court', was written in the Irish language and was for many years accessible only to those who could read that tongue; for although an English translation existed, it was banned in Ireland — presumably by a non-Irish speaking censor. In time more liberal principles prevailed, and the poem is now available to all, while the poet himself is honoured annually and vociferously by the Merriman Summer School.

Feakle
His grave is on the other side of the county at Feakle, a foothill village in the Slieve Aughty Mountains, where he spent many years and chose as the setting for his epic poem. The village was also the home of the witch or wise woman, Biddy Early, whose cottage has been restored and whose life provided Lady Gregory with material for her 'Visions and Beliefs of the West of Ireland'.

The Coast to Loop Head
Further down the coast from Enristymon are the small villages of Milltown Malbay and Quilty, and then there is a natural stopping-place

Munster

at Kilkee which, apart from its popularity as a holiday resort, has interesting surroundings. The Duggerna Rocks to the west hold natural bathing pools and a large natural amphitheatre hollowed out by the sea with rock strata forming seats.

Beyond Kilkee a long road reaches out to Loop Head which is the south-westerly extremity of County Clare: from here it is possible to look back to Kerry and the MacGillycuddy Reeks in the south, and to the north as far as the mountains of Connemara. Standing off from the headland an isolated cliff segment is known as the rock of the legendary Irish lovers, Diarmiud and Grainne; the channel isolating the Rock is called 'Lover's Leap' in this case a reluctant lover in the person of Cuchulainn who jumped across from the mainland to escape some poor girl's amorous attention.

North Shore of the Shannon
The Shannon enters the sea at Loop Head, and travelling inland along its northern shore the big market town of Kilrush is the landing point for ferryboats crossing the river from Limerick; from Cappagh Pier boats go out to Scattery Island which has numerous church ruins, dating from as early as the 9th century, and a fine Round Tower. About five miles away Ellen Hanly — the 'Colleen Bawn' — is buried in the graveyard of Killimer Church. Her body was washed up here after her murder on a boat and interred by a local schoolmaster; since then souvenir-hunters have chipped away the tombstone so assiduously that to date it has had to be replaced three times.

As the road moves deeper into the shelter of the estuary, the countryside becomes more domesticated and there is a pretty stretch near the village of Kildysart which looks out towards a host of islands; from here it is an easy run into Ennis which is the capital of the county.

Ennis
A comfortable town on the River Fergus, Ennis has some handsome Georgian houses, the ruins of a Franciscan friary which flourished as a seat of learning between the 13th and 15th centuries, a fine courthouse with an impressive Ionic portico, and more than its share of monuments. There is one to the Liberator, Daniel O'Connell, another called The Maid of 'Erin' to three patriots executed in Manchester in 1867 and, larger than lifesize like the man himself, a memorial to the controversial Eamon de Valera who refused to accept the provisions of the Treaty of 1922 and dragged the country into civil war. Clare was his constituency and he retained his seat in the east of the county from 1917 until he became President of Ireland in 1959.

East Clare Castles
This part of Clare is castle country, and it is in this area that so much

enterprising work has gone into restoring historic old buildings and putting them to work again. At Knappogue, where an elaborate crenellated 19th-century addition skirts the front of the old Norman keep, 'mediaeval' banquets are served; in the grounds of the restored 15th-century Craggaunowen Castle a full-scale model of a Bronze Age *crannóg* lake dwelling has been built; Dromoland Castle has been turned into a rather too luxurious hotel, while Bunratty, on the main road from Shannon Airport into Limerick, is the best known of all.

Bunratty Castle
It is thought that Bunratty originally stood on an island site and may have been fortified by the Vikings. Certainly it was rebuilt several times during the Norman period, and the present fortress dates from the 15th century. Ruined and derelict, it was bought by Lord Gort in 1945 and has been magnificently restored and furnished: there is a vast dining hall on the first floor where more mediaeval banquets are served with entertainment to match. The approach is from outside by a wooden staircase, and above there is a great hall typical of the period, as well as a small chapel and living quarters.

In the old days a town surrounded the castle, but in this modern age Bunratty's immediate neighbour is a jolly little pub with the startling name of 'Dirty Nelly's'.

There is an excellent folk park and museum in the castle grounds, and here 'traditional evenings' are built around a hearty meal of Irish Stew, with singing and dancing and story-telling to boot. In recent years an entire 19th-century village street has been reconstructed and keeps busy with the practise of traditional crafts, while a first-class restaurant operates in the mews attached to the handsome manor of Bunratty House.

Killaloe: Brian Boru
Clare is bounded on the east by the Shannon and at the foot of its first great lake, Lough Derg, lies the prettiest town in the whole of the county. Sheltered by gentle mountain slopes and looking out over the water, Killaloe has narrow, hilly streets and a lovely bridge with thirteen graceful arches. There was a church here in the 6th century, and the present cathedral was founded on the site towards the end of the 12th century; near an earlier Romanesque door stands a stone with inscriptions in both *ogham* and Viking runes. In the cathedral grounds is a well-preserved little Romanesque church with a stone roof, while further up the hill is St Molua's Oratory which was rescued from an island due to be submerged in the flooding of the Shannon Hydro-Electric Scheme.

Brian Boru was born near Killaloe, possibly at the ring-fort of *Beal Boru* where an ancient timber house was uncovered by excavations some years ago. His palace of Kincora was in the district also, but even in Ireland where categoric insistence so often gives myth the status of history, no one has yet succeeded in identifying the site — or sites.

County Tipperary

Tipperary is a big, prosperous inland farming county with the illusion of a coastline created by the eastern shore of Lough Derg. The centre of the county is a wide, fertile plain watered by the River Suir and its tributaries, with the rich Golden Vale of Ireland spreading out tranquilly towards Limerick. In the south the Galtee Mountains and the Knockmealdowns rise in rounded slopes, serene and handsome, to provide good climbing and walking country with none of the menacing character of the ranges near the Atlantic.

By and large, the landscapes of Tipperary are man-made, domesticated and civilised, with evidence of the fine settlements dating back to Early and pre-Christian times to demonstrate that no one who set eyes on it was ever in any doubt about the worth of this country.

Northern Tipperary

Rather like Yorkshire, County Tipperary is divided into two 'ridings', the northern administered by the town of Nenagh, which has a mediaeval castle with a circular keep, and, in the County Gaol complex, a heritage centre illustrating 'Lifestyles in North West Tipperary'.

Roscrea, Damer House

North-east of Nenagh is Roscrea, one of the most important religious centres of Ireland during Early Christian and mediaeval times. More than 200 standing stones in the neighbourhood suggest a matching position in the pre-Christian era too. The present town owes its origin to a 7th-century monastic foundation, and was the source of the 8th-century Book of Dimma which contains the four Gospels. A Round Tower in reasonable condition and the remains of monasteries that flourished between the 12th and 16th centuries may still be seen, but perhaps the most spectacular historic building in Roscrea today is the Damer House.

Built in the court of a 13th-century Norman castle, it is an impressive example of an early 18th-century town house. A staircase of carved pinewood forms a magnificent centrepiece, and antique Irish furniture has been assembled in the rooms. There is a heritage centre in an adjacent annex.

Devil's Bit Mountain

The road south to Thurles passes by Templemore in the shadow of the Devil's Bit Mountain with the notable gap created when His Dark Majesty bit off a piece. According to legend, the morsel was not to his liking so he spat it out on the plains to the south where it formed the Rock of Cashel and was certainly exorcised of any lingering satanic contamination by the arrival of St Patrick. Those subscribing to this account will do well to ignore the unpalatable fact that the 'Bit' is of sandstone and the Rock of limestone.

Holy Cross Abbey; Thurles
The largest mediaeval monastery in the country was said to be Athassel, but today the ruins of Holy Cross Abbey near Thurles are more striking and preserve one of the rare wall paintings to survive in Ireland from the past. Founded in the 12th century Holy Cross was much extended in the 15th when pilgrimages were made to venerate the fragment of the True Cross enshrined there. It has recently been restored and is once again in use as a church. In the town of Thurles there are the ruins of two Norman fortresses, but these are dwarfed by the immensely high campanile of the cathedral. To the east lie the remains of Kilcooly Abbey.

Cashel
The most impressive settlement of all was at Cashel, where a dramatic limestone rock, crowned with secular and religious buildings, dominates the flat countryside for miles around.

Originally a seat of the kings of Munster, Cashel was strongly fortified under the rule of Aengus when St Patrick arrived around 450 AD. He promptly converted the king and his court, and in the course of the baptismal ceremony inadvertently drove his crozier through the royal foot; assuming this to be a vital part of the initiation ritual, the monarch bore the thrust without comment, and church and state went forward hand-in-hand into history — though the latter probably limped a little in his progress.

St Patrick made Cashel a bishopric, but in the early days incumbents of the office were as apt to wield the sword as the crozier. Viking raids were beaten off time and again, and in 908 Cormac Mac Cuilleannain, who combined the disciplines of spiritual and temporal authority with that of scholasticism, got himself killed trying to become High King of Ireland. Some seventy years later Brian Boru was crowned High King at Cashel and made it his capital.

Romanesque Chapel
At the beginning of the 12th century the Rock was handed over exclusively to the Church, and ecclesiastical building began in earnest. The bishop, Cormac MacCarthy, started with a chapel for himself, and this remarkable Romanesque building still stands in reasonably good repair, its square flanking towers revealing the influence of German visitors who had been sent a few years earlier by Dionysius,

the inappropriately-named Abbot of Ratisbon, to collect money for his church. History repeated itself to an extent recently with the arrival of a German-speaking Swiss who has set up an excellent restaurant in the abandoned Wesleyan chapel at the foot of the Rock.

Cathedral

A Round Tower was built at the same time as Cormac's Chapel, and in 1152 Cashel became an archbishopric. A new cathedral was built on the site of an earlier one in the 13th century and later a fortified residential tower was added. The need for such precautions was tellingly demonstrated in 1495 when the Earl of Kildare set fire to the cathedral because, he explained to the King, he thought the archbishop was inside. The 15th-century Hall of the Vicars Choral, which housed the clergy and minor canons attached to the see, is just inside the modern entrance to Cashel. In front of it stands a seven-foot cross with carvings of the Crucifixion and of St Patrick.

Priory and Palace

Inevitably, the splendour of Cashel spilled over into the town beneath and the surrounding countryside: notably at the foot of the Rock in the ruins of a 15th-century Dominican priory which retains a window from the 13th century. By the 18th century however Cashel was firmly in Protestant hands, and in 1730 the archbishop of the time added to its ecclesiastical splendour by building himself a handsome new palace in the centre of the town. It is now a hotel, Michelin-starred for its food, and worth a visit on that account as much as for the fine panelling and plasterwork that have been zealously preserved in the large hall. Another hotel is housed in a historic old tower dwelling, called 'Grant's Castle' and serves more modest fare, including a Tourist menu priced at IR£5.60 and IR£7.50.

Hore Abbey

Further off, in a tranquil field west of the Rock, stand the ruins of Hore Abbey which was built for Benedictine monks but later handed over to the Cistercians.

Southern Tipperary

Fethard; Kilthane

South of Cashel in the village of Fethard — which stands in pleasant country beneath the conical mountain of Slievenamon — there are the well-preserved remains of an Augustinian priory. All the surrounding foundations must have known the influence of Cashel in their time, but there is evidence of temporal power as well. In Fethard, which was once a place of considerable importance, three 15th-century keeps are still standing, while three miles away Kiltinane castle overhangs the Glashawley river on its rocky promotory. Re-built after Cromwell's cannon had damaged it severely, it has walls of immense thickness with three corner towers; the first-floor ceilings are vaulted, and from the courtyard a stepped passage leads down to a fortified well.

Cahir

The greatest castle of all in Tipperary is, however, at Cahir, where a massive 15th-century fortress stands on a rocky island beside a bridge across the Suir. It is protected by a strong outer wall with turrets and inside the area is divided into two enclosures, one of them containing a three-storey tower.

Cahir itself is an attractive little town on the main road from Dublin to Cork. The local hotel, Cahir House, is pleasant and unpretentious and has a very pretty garden where tea is often served in summer. Cahir marks the turning-off point for the Glen of Atherlow beneath the Galtee Mountains; one road running north-west to the Glen and Tipperary town, another skirting the southern side of the Galtee range, to go towards Cork, via Mitchelstown.

Mitchelstown Caves

The Mitchelstown caves may be explored with the assistance of a guide. They comprise two complexes, both heavily encrusted with dripstone formations: the 'new' cave was discovered only in the 19th century, but the Desmond Cave, for which rope or ladder is required in the descent, was known at least as far back as 1601 when the *Sugan,* or 'Straw', Earl of Desmond hid there from the English.

Clonmel

The southern part of the county is administered from Clonmel, a town deriving considerable architectural interest from the turreted gateway which arches above the main street and from its classical Main Guard, but its most important attribute in Irish eyes is its association with the greyhound. The passion for greyhound-racing extends into the neighbouring counties of Kilkenny, Wexford and Waterford, but its fervent core is in Tipperary, and in Clonmel in particular: it would be a poor evening when the country roads around this pleasant town were not peopled by breeders, exercising the slender animals as many as half-a-dozen at a time.

Carrick-on-Suir

From Clonmel a minor road branches west to join a southern route across the Knockmealdown Mountains and through the 'Vee' down into County Waterford. A main road runs east beside the river, through pretty country to Carrick-on-Suir which has a picturesque situation in the river valley. Its old West Gate has a clock tower on top, and near the ruins of a 15th-century Ormonde castle stands a fine gabled Elizabethan house which is now being restored. The house was built by the tenth Earl of Ormonde, 'Black Tom', to receive Queen Elizabeth, who never came, and there is a story that the Queen's mother, Anne Boleyn, a daughter of one of the Butler ladies, was born in the old

Munster

castle which is now in ruins.

County Waterford

Waterford City

Despite constant harassment by native Irish tribes, the Danes kept a firm grip on Waterford city until the Normans arrived. Even today their influence survives in some place-names and in the occasional use of 'Olaf' as a Christian name: more notably in Reginald's Tower, a stout, rounded keep on the quayside, which is said to have been built by Reginald the Dane in 1003 but was almost certainly reconstructed by the Normans in the 13th century.

What the Irish failed to achieve in 300 years, Raymond le Gros accomplished in a matter of days and handed over the beaten city to Strongbow — who immediately consolidated his position as conquerer by marrying King Dermot MacMurrough's daughter, Eva, in Reginald's Tower. From that time on Waterford was a bulwark of the Pale, second only to Dublin in importance, and as a loyal city was glad to welcome in succession Henry II, King John — who gave it its first charter — and Richard II.

With a sure instinct for choosing the winning side, Waterford remained loyal to Henry VII during the attempts to place first Lambert Simnel and then Perkin Warbeck on the English throne. Much honour and affluence resulted from the prudence. Thereafter, however, religion got the upper hand, and Waterford lost its charter for its refusal to acknowledge the supremacy of the Crown in spiritual matters. It chose the losing side again during the Cromwellian wars and after repulsing the Protector's seige in 1649 was taken by one of the generals a year later. James II was received there on his way to Kinsale after the Battle of the Boyne, but when he had departed William of Orange forced the city to surrender.

Reginald's Tower

Today Waterford is a small seaport of considerable character, approached by a 700-foot bridge across the River Suir. The quays are lively with small shipping and the commercial appurtenances thereof, and on the corner of the Mall Reginald's Tower still stands, with its four-foot thick walls as redoubtable as ever. In its time it has served as a mint and later as a prison, but now there is a Tourist

Right: Currachs on the Aran Islands
Poulnabrone Dolmen, Co. Clare
Overleaf: Aran Islands ferries, Inishmore
The Dingle Peninsula, Co. Kerry

Office in the base while the upper floor is devoted to a permanent exhibition; this includes a charter roll dating from 1394 and the civic regalia presented to the city by Henry VIII. There is a fine view of the city from the roof of the Tower.

The Mall
In the Mall the classical style of the late 18th-century Town Hall is supported by the characteristic Irish Georgian doors and fanlights of houses nearby. The Mall itself is divided between the usual municipal offices and a pretty little red-plush theatre, and here the Waterford Light Opera Festival goes on in September. This full-throated event is unique in its amateur status and attracts musical societies from England and Wales as well as Ireland.

Churches and Cathedral
Some of the old Norman fortifications may still be seen in Waterford and the tower of a 13th-century Franciscan friary still stands in the 'French Church', so called after the Huguenot refugees who used it in the 18th century. The Catholic Cathedral has gold and silver vessels dating from the 17th and 18th centries, and in St Olaf's Church, which was founded by the Danes, re-built by the Normans and then re-built again in the 18th century, there is a pulpit and episcopal throne of carved black oak. The back streets and laneways of the city are full of chance echoes of the past, but in the main Waterford is, and likes to be known as, a modern industrial city whose principal claim to manufacturing fame is, of course, glass.

Glass manufacture
The manufacture of glass began in Waterford in the 18th century. It reached its peak in the decades spanning the end of that century and the beginning of the next, and the magnificent examples of the work of this period may be seen in the Town Hall. The glass factory closed in 1861, but was started up again in 1947 and now employs some 1,200 craftsmen who are hard put to keep up with a huge volume of orders from all over the world. Visitors are welcome at the works, which are like the setting for a Gothic fairytale with their incandescant furnaces and the noise and movement of glass being blown and worked by hand into all kinds of shapes and forms.

West to Comeragh Mountains
Waterford is not a large city, and it is easy to get out of it and explore the gentle hinterland around. Only a few miles away are the grounds

Previous page: Portnoo, Co. Donegal
Dunluce Castle, Co. Antrim
Left: The Giant's Causeway, Co. Antrim

Munster

and gardens of 18th-century Mount Congreve, and a little further on along the banks of the River Clodiagh, is the village of Portlaw which was founded by Quakers in the 19th century.

Curraghamore
Curraghamore, seat of the Marquis of Waterford, is just beside the village, and with the Comeragh Mountains rising behind it forms one of the most beautiful demesnes in the country; the extraordinary shell house in the grounds was made by a Lady Beresford of the 18th century. The gardens are sometimes open to the public, but times vary and it is wise to check with the local tourist information office in advance. On the other side of the bridge at Portlaw, Fiddown Chapel with its classical monuments shows signs of excellent restoration by the Irish Georgian Society.

Rathgormack
The Comeragh Mountains are amongst the most attractive and easily explored in the country, and their northern side is particularly popular with walkers. The small, tranquil village of Rathgormack in this area has the remains of a mediaeval church with fortified tower, and a little way off at Milvate, a small Bronze Age chamber tomb.

South and West Waterford
Waterford Harbour
Three rivers — the Nore, the Barrow and the Suir — flow into the head of Waterford Harbour and on together to the sea. The long harbour coastline curves capriciously around the harbour mouth to Passage East, a nice, old-fashioned little village at the foot of a steep hill where the ferryboat leaves for Ballyhack on the Wexford side. From Cheekpoint Hill, a couple of miles north, there is an excellent view of the surrounding countryside showing mountains and headlands and the city spires of Waterford.

The road from Passage goes on towards the sea past Geneva Barracks where a company of Swiss goldsmiths settled briefly in the 18th century; their building was taken over for use as a barracks and many of the 1798 insurgents were imprisoned there. Woodstown Strand by the roadside further on has a pretty backing of trees, and then the road comes to Dunmore East, which is a picturesque little cove sheltered by cliffs and headlands, ideal for secluded summer holidays.

Tramore
From Dunmore a winding road leads back to Waterford via the big seaside town of Tramore. With its huge sandy beach, its promenade and its amusement facilities, Tranmore is a highly-developed holiday resort and reaches the climax of its season in race week. Those in search of peace and quiet, however, will be best advised to go a little further west to the small, unspoiled villages of Annestown,

Bunmahon, Clonea or Stradbally.

Dungarvan
There is fine rock scenery, interspersed with coves and beaches, all the way along from Tramore to Dungarvan, where the coast bends in to form the harbour mouth of the county's administrative centre — the county only, though, for Waterford city is a law unto itself. Dungarven and the area around it is still called the 'Decies' from the *Deise* tribe from County Meath, which is said to have settled there around 200 AD. King John built a now ruined castle there near the end of the 12th century, but until the 19th century, when the Duke of Devonshire had a causeway laid, the town was divided by the River Colligan and such citizens as had occasion to go from east to west about their business simply paddled across or waited for the ferry.

Some fragments of the old walls remain along the 'Dead Walk' in Dungarvan, and in the churchyard there is a curious perforated 'gable' for which no explanation has yet been found. Beside the river on the eastern side of the town are the remains of a 13th-century Augustinian foundation, and near them the west wall of MacGrath's Castle which dates from the same period. The MacGraths were a prominent local family in their time, and striking evidence of their influence may be seen in the Master MacGrath memorial a few miles along the road outside the town. The limestone monument to this celebrated greyhound, who was defeated only once in his public racing career, reduces the *ogham* stones at Drumlohane and Kiltera, the dolmens and megalithic tombs in the east of the county — Ballynageeragh, Knockeen, Gaulstown and Matthewstown — to the proper perspective of mere primitive achievement.

Helvick Head
The main road to the west has a turning-off for Helvick Head, which crowns the outer arm of Dungarven Harbour and gives a fine view back along the coast towards Tramore. It is possible to follow a minor road below the Drum Hills along the coast to Ardmore, where the ruins of an Early Christian foundation rises above a fine beach. This monastic settlement was established by St Declan who, it is rumoured, got to the site before St Patrick and did not take altogether kindly to the Apostle's arrival and his Romish ways. No sign of dissension is revealed now, however, in the remains of the little oratory or the hermitage church in the Round Tower or in the cathedral which covers various architectural styles from the 10th to the 14th centuries. A large glacial boulder lying on the beach is said to be the craft by which the saint sailed to Ireland.

Lismore
Lismore may be approached from either Dungarvan or Ardmore, the former being the principal road. This tiny village in a pretty corner of the Blackwater Valley is completely dominated by the castle which

Munster

stands on a cliff above the river. It is believed to stand on the site of an early monastery — which may well be true, for in its day Lismore was a mighty bastion of learning in the Christian world, and though only the graceful 17th-century cathedral of the Church of Ireland still remains, the written records confirming the eminence of the former monastic city are supported by the great Lismore Crozier and by the 15th-century Book of Lismore, both of which were discovered in the castle walls early in the last century.

The present castle incorporates a mediaeval fortress built by Prince John in 1185. Sir Walter Raleigh had it towards the end of the 16th century and sold it to the 'Great' Earl of Cork, whose son, born in the castle, was the perpetrator of Boyle's Law. Late in the 18th century it passed into the hands of the Dukes of Devonshire, who are responsible for its present massive form, its splendid appointments and its excellent upkeep.

Several 17th-century features are visible in the castle gardens, which are open to the public. The walls and towers at the western end date from 1626-7 and proved of vital significance in the seige of 1642. The Riding House, which divides the upper and lower gardens, was built in 1631, and the wall connecting it to the castle a year later. The Yew Walk at Lismore Castle is considered one of the finest in these islands, and outside the walled garden the woodlands favour the growth of magnolias and camellias.

River-Valley Tours

There are lovely river-valley tours to be made in the countryside around Lismore, but the best road of all leads up through the Knockmealdown Mountains to the 'Vee' and on to Clonmel and Kilkenny. At Cappoquin there is a turning off for Mount Melleray where Trappist monks maintain themselves on farmland created out of barren moor, and provide a centre of religious retreat for the laity.

Dunguaire Castle, Co. Galway

Connacht

'To hell or to Connacht' was the choice offered the Irish driven off their estates by Cromwell in the 17th century. In fact, the country immediately west of the Shannon has plenty of land worth husbanding, but getting on for the Atlantic there is little scope for agricultural livelihood. The Irish went, however, and it is often claimed that the tinkers who wander the western roads today — many of them with bright red or fair hair — are the descendants of well-to-do gentry expelled from the fat pastures of the east long ago.

Wild and barren and forlorn, the further west, the more inhospitable the land becomes; and by the familiar paradox prevailing in such contexts, the more beautiful and emotive. In the days of Conn of the Hundred Battles this was proud terrain and powerful, but in recent centuries the people have scrabbled for a meagre living from the sea and the hard, stony soil. Only within the past fifty years have government agencies begun to improve their lot, largely through the influence of tourism.

But while State-directed tourist development has been far-sighted and properly mindful of the integrity of the landscapes, it is in this part of the country that the passion for quasi-Spanish domestic architecture is at its most unbridled. Patios and open archways proliferate amongst the startling white bungalows and, where it occurs, the indigenous thatched cottage is more likely to prove a custom-built holiday home than a native dwelling.

It might be argued that at least the single-storey elevation of the Irish 'hacienda' is in keeping with cottage tradition. But the vivid tiled roofs and Moorish *kitsch* are sorely incompatible with the misty landscapes of Connemara, and inevitably give rise to wry speculation about their possible function in a climate rarely conducive to outdoor living. The best to be hoped for is a rapid weathering process.

County Galway

Kinvara to Galway
The approach to Galway from the south is through flat country with low stone walls flung together over centuries of land clearance. The road runs along the wide mouth of Galway Bay to Kinvara and the dramatic spectacle of Dun Guaire Castle standing on a low rocky promontory in the sea.

Dun Guaire Castle
Restored as a dwelling house, the castle provides mediaeval banquets during the tourist season, and entertainment — although the latter can hardly hope to equal the legendary occasion in the 7th century when King Guaire and his court sat down to dinner, only to see the entire meal rise from the table, dishes and all, and fly out of the window.

The King and his companions gave chase on horseback and caught up with the repast in the next county, where St Colman MacDuagh was just finishing a seven-year fast. The King watched, quite literally dumbfounded it seems, while the saint demolished the lot, then all gave thanks for the miracle and kingly lands were handed over for the establishment of a monastery in County Galway. The present remains at Kilmacduagh, however, date mostly from the 13th century; they include a Round Tower and churches, the former leaning dubiously to one side.

Clarinbridge; Kilcolgan
The road north from Kinvara passes by two villages with famous pubs closely associated with the Galway Oyster Festival. The late Mr.

Paddy Burke, whose tavern still thrives in Clarinbridge, was one of the founders of the Festival, while at Moran's of the Weir in Kilcolgan, ritual demands that the first oyster of the year be presented to the Mayor of Galway by the pretty girl chosen as 'Oyster Pearl' and Queen of the festival. The Spanish Arch in Galway city also plays a central part in the festival, which occupies three days and the best part of three nights early in September, and has been known to convince even the French that the marriage of Guinness and oysters was made in heaven. Its only equal in local esteem is the famous Galway Race Week.

From Clarinbridge it is a short drive through Oranmore to Galway and the sea-side suburb of Salthill. Christopher Columbus is believed to have attended Mass in the Church of St Nicholas before setting out for America, and the building, now dedicated to the Protestant faith, survives with many additions and amendments, from the 14th century.

Galway City

In the past Galway traded extensively with Spain, and some slight traces of this heritage remain, notably in the Spanish Arch near the old fish market. More vivid in local memory, however, are the 'Tribes' who harried the city ferociously for years, and the inscription over the vanished West Gate is still quoted: 'From the fury of the O'Flahertys, good Lord deliver us.'

The Lord, however, delivered them their share of vicissitudes in the course of a turbulent history, though the fury without seems to have been matched by the equal passion within. In 1493 a mayor of Galway, James Lynch, hanged his own son for the murder of a Spanish guest, and a later inscription on a wall of an old jail records the deed. Such drastic pruning notwithstanding, the Lynch family provided more than eighty lords mayor for the city, and 14th-century Lynch Castle still stands, though now occupied by the offices of a bank.

Architecture
The Castle, the Courthouse and the Franciscan church are the most distinguished buildings in Galway, for the picturesque thatched cottages of the Claddagh have been replaced by uninspired modern dwellings, and the traditions represented by this little fishing community survive only in the Claddagh wedding-ring, a thin gold band forming two hands which hold the heart. The past comes alive, however, at the *Taidhbhearc*, Galway's small and successful Irish-language theatre which has been the training-ground of several Abbey actors and producers, while the more recent Druid theatre group is now attracting international attention.

Salmon Weir
Lake Corrib, which divides the relatively prosperous region of east

111

Connacht

Galway from Connemara, drains into the sea through the city, and at the Salmon Weir Bridge countless salmon may be seen resting before their assault on the weir on their way upstream. Beyond the bridge stands the modern Roman Catholic cathedral, remarkable for its size and conglomeration of architectural styles.

Eastern Galway

Tuam

Tuam and Ballinasloe are the most important towns in east County Galway. The former has a fine Market Cross dating from the 12th century, and a much re-built cathedral incorporating a Norman arch. In the vicinity, beside the village of Headford, lie the extensive friary ruins of Ross Errilly, and due south, beside a lake, the remains of Knockmoy Abbey where a faded frescoe survives from mediaeval times. East of Tuam is the site of an ancient *crannóg*, or lake dwelling, while on the south-east road to Barnnaderg, Ballinderry Castle sports a *sheela-na-gig* on the keystone over its doorway.

Ballinasloe

Ballinasloe is a big, cheerful country town built around a large square which sizzles with life and noise and pungent farm smells during the five-day horse and cattle fair in October. For the rest of the year the town is quiet enough and makes a good base for excursions to the antiquities of the area. At Kilconnell there are the ruins of a Franciscan friary and also a marvellous low stone bridge with square arches which hardly clear the water; at Clontuskert the remains of an Augustinian abbey, the abbot of which was accused of harbouring prostitutes and homicides during the 15th century; and close to the banks of the Shannon, in the neighbourhood of a 16th-century tower and a church with a wooden statue dating from the 14th century, are the ruins of Romanesque Clonfert Cathedral.

Southern Galway

Athenry

The principal towns in south Galway are Athenry and Loughrea, with the former, as the stronghold of Norman power in the county, boasting more than its share of historic remains. These include massive town walls dating from the beginning of the 14th century, 13th-century castle walls and towers with gables added in the 17th, a Market Cross in the 'tabernacle' style more common in southern England, and in the ruins of the Dominican Priory several grave-slabs bearing illustrations of the trades practised by the men buried beneath.

Loughrea

In Loughrea the ruins of an ancient priory are challenged by fine modern stained-glass in the present cathedral, while a few miles north of the town stands the Turoe Stone which is considered the finest example of *La Tène* art in Ireland.

Gort

The vicinity of Gort, which was once the seat of that same monarch who chased his dinner about the countryside, is associated with the Irish Literary Renaissance of the early 20th century: Lady Gregory lived nearby at Coole Park, and just a few miles away the poet Yeats settled for a while in a 16th-century tower beside a stream. Yeats restored Thoor Ballylee when he lived there, but it fell into disrepair after his departure in 1929 and stayed in that condition until its more recent restoration as a museum to his memory. Lough Cutra with its wooded islets is not far away, and was as much admired for its pretty scenery in Yeats's time as it is today.

Connemara

The land west of Lake Corrib is painfully poor. Great tracks of lake and mountain and moorland stretch out to the heavily-indented rock of the coastline, which then splinters away into dozens of tiny islands. This is Connemara, and it has a desolate and heart-breaking beauty, combined incongruously with excellent roads to enable the traveller to explore its sad loveliness at will.

Ring Road to Clifden

A ring road follows the coastline west from Galway city, past the small seaside village of Spiddal, then north to the mouth of Cashla Bay into Costelloe; here a sub-system of minor roads wanders off to a group of lonely little islands, culminating in the dark tower marking Golam Head. The main road goes on through Screeb and Gortmore along the shores of Kilkieran Bay to Carna. The islands in Lough Skannive near here bear a resemblance to the ancient fortified lake-dwellings known as *crannógs*, while off-shore on St MacDara's Island there is an early Christian church built of unusually large stones. Local boatmen take visitors out to the island, and in the old days passing fishermen used to dip their sails three times in honour of the saint.

The road winds north again, along Bertraghboy Bay, to Cashel, which looks out across sparkling sea to a host of tiny islands. The local manor here was converted into an hotel some years back and housed President de Gaulle during his visit to Ireland; a few miles inland, in lush wooded country altogether unlike the rugged terrain of the coast, Ballinachinch Castle also serves 20th-century needs as an hotel.

Clifden

The coast road continues on around the next headland, through Roundstone and Ballyconneely Bay, north to Ballinaboy and Clifden — which, with its bracing climate and picturesque situation between mountains and sea, is considered the capital of Connemara. It is a lively place, popular for holidays, and at its liveliest during the Connemara Pony Show in August. These sturdy little animals are native to the region, gentle and friendly and much in demand with breeders and riding teachers. There are strands and sandy coves in

113

the vicinity, and what Thackeray described as 'the most beautiful districts it is ever the fortune of a traveller to examine.' A spur road runs out to the fishing village of Cleggan where boats come and go from Inishbofin Island.

North to Leenane
Working north through Letterfrack, which is so often vivid with wild fuschia, another spur goes off the Renvyle, and here a long, low hotel, which was once the home of Oliver St John Gogarty, looks out across tranquil sands to the little islands off-shore. The main road goes on to green, wooded Kylemore with its castellated abbey — now a girls' school and a favoured subject for picture postcards — and then runs for ten miles between the formidable heights of the Maamturk Mountains and the deep, narrow waters of Killary Harbour; the steep mountain walls of Mweelrea in Mayo rise on the other side, and at the head of the bay the secluded little village of Leenane marks the turning-off for the northerly county.

Joyce County to Oughterard
The ring road divides in two to travel through the Joyce County back to Galway; out between mountains, with Lough Nafooey on one side and Lough Mask on the other to Clonbur and Cornamona, or straight down between the heights to Maam Cross. Here the roads join together again and make their way along the shore of Lough Corrib to Oughterard, where boats may be hired to explore the great lake and its islands. In the near vicinity a handsomely-restored fortress of the O'Flaherty family rises six storeys from its rock foundation to dominate the surrounding country as it has done since the 15th century.

Lough Corrib
Measuring sixty-eight square miles in all, Lough Corrib is the second largest lake in Ireland and a celebrated water for both game fishing and coarse angling. It offers particularly good sport when the mayfly rises, but even those who cannot distinguish one end of a rod from another will find it worthwhile to hire a boat out to the lake island of Inchagoill, which means the 'Island of the Stranger'. The antiquities here include ecclesiastical remains from the time of St Patrick, another church from the 10th century and an obelisk incised with Roman characters which are said to be the oldest Christian inscription outside the catacombs.

Oughterard to Clifden — Mountain Route
From Oughterard a fine road bisects Connemara, running back out by Maam Cross through splendid scenery to Recess, where the green Connemara marble is quarried; then on in the spectacular shadow of the Twelve Bens to Clifden. Other roads branch off for the coast at various points, the loveliest being the northern route from Recess which passes between the Bens and Maamturk Mountains on its way to Kylemore.

The Aran Islands

Although they belong to County Galway, the Aran Islands are, in fact, the last visible outcrop of the stern limestone region of the Burren in Clare. Their western faces rise in fierce cliffs above the Atlantic, but the land tilts more gently towards the water on the mainland side. There are hardly any trees on the islands, and it seems illogical to expect fields either, but over the centuries the islanders have 'made' their land, wedging crevices in the limestone and spreading sand and seaweed to create a soil which supports crops and also provides grazing for first-class cattle. Ingenious are the uses of adversity, and even today fields are laboriously cleared by hand and the rocks and stones piled into low stone walls with hardly ever a gate. It is the custom on the two smaller islands simply to kick down a wall to release cattle, then build it up again to pen them in.

Prehistoric forts

It is not known when this splendidly stubborn practise of 'making' the land began, but certainly the islands have been inhabited for a very long time indeed. Enormous prehistoric stone forts, the dates and origins of which have never been definitely established, are evidence of very early civilisation. Legend has it that these were built by the survivors of the same Firbolgs who were routed at Moytura and it is as good a story as any: without doubt the builders of Dun Aengus were determined never to let their enemies get within arm's reach if massive stone defences could prevent it.

Early Christians

The Early Christians are heavily represented, too, by a wealth of crosses and churches, but the history of the islands up to the 19th century remains obscure, with only occasional recorded comment to substantiate the theoretical claims of stones and monuments.

Aran Sweaters

This was a community apart, isolated by heavy seas which permitted only occasional trips by hooker into Galway. While the native language vanished from all but a few parishes on the mainland, the islanders continued to speak Irish — and still do amongst themselves, although they are now equally fluent in English. And it was on Aran that the *bainín* sweater, now a high-fashion garment, evolved, the elaborate patterns in thick, uncured wool being designed so that the bodies of drowned fishermen might be identified when they were washed ashore long afterwards. Nowhere else in Ireland has change been so long in coming, and although the Aran Islands are moving into the 20th century — with an air service from the mainland and landing strips on each of the islands — there is still something left of the life dramatised by Synge in 'Riders to the Sea', and by Robert Flaherty in his epic documentary, 'Man of Aran'.

Connacht

Getting to the Islands
Despite the services of Aer Árann the best way to visit the islands is still by the mail boat which ploughs out thirty miles through the sea from Galway, carrying a highly-articulate cargo of tourists, returning islanders, livestock and assorted parcels. There is a pier at Kilronan on Inishmore, the biggest island, but harbour facilities at Inishmaan and Inishmore are so slight that the boat is forced to moor out at sea, and passengers, goods and cattle complete the journey by *curragh*.

These long, light canoe-style boats of tarred canvas stretched over laths are more seaworthy than they look. They have been used by the island fleets for centuries and are remarkably agile: propelled by three experienced sets of tapered oars, they can race through the water with the speed and elegance of a shark, yet are sufficiently sturdy to withstand the struggles of cattle being towed ashore. This is a rather grisly operation, for the only method of embarking any sizeable livestock for the two smaller islands is to winch them down over the side of the mailboat into the water; the head of the animal is then held firmly against the stern of the *curragh* and willy or nilly the rest of the beast swims along behind.

Inishmore
Inishmore is the capital of the Aran Islands: with resident doctor and priest as well as a road fit for cars, it ranks as a near-metropolis beside Inisheer and Inishmaan. For all that, however, it has not been spoiled, and the road beyond the harbour village of Kilronan leads through a stern countryside, spectacular with the ruins of earlier civilisation. There are several dramatic stone forts, of which the greatest, Dun Aengus towers above a 300-foot sheer cliff drop to the sea. Its formidable inner ramparts, which include small chambers in the innermost wall, are protected by a *chevaux-de-frise* of primitive workmanship but sophisticated concept, and the whole complex forms a vast semi-circle open to the Atlantic gales on its western side. Each of the islands has its fortresses, but Dun Aengus is unmatched for sheer barbaric bulk and splendour.

Inisheer
Inisheer is the prettiest and friendliest of the three islands, and also the poorest. It has an immense sandy beach which must be crossed laboriously and with high steps, to reach the village above. Again, there are forts and early churches, and here also a mediaeval castle; but the charm of the place is in the grace and hospitality of the people who will gladly invite a civil stranger indoors for a cup of strong tea and a slice of the marvellous brown bread baking on the fire. Huge families live in the small cottages, for it is the traditionally high birth-rate that has kept the population of the Aran Islands stable despite emigration; and despite the growing influence of Dublin and London and the visitors from New York, the islanders seem content enough

with the harsh and simple standards of their daily life.

Inishmaan

Inishmaan, by contrast, is a stranger place and rather reserved in its dealings with the outside world. The people are courteous but not unduly friendly, hospitable in accordance with ancient custom but known for their ability to strike a hard bargain where business is concerned; and to them posing for photographs for tourists is, quite properly, a commercial business and requires a fee.

Here the traditional long red flannel skirt and black shawl are still worn by some of the older women, while a number of the men still dress in sleeveless tweed jackets over their *baínín* jerseys, loose trousers held up by a bright, woven sash called a *crios* and flat, heel-less slippers of hide which are known as 'pampooties'. Synge lived on Inishmaan and wrote a book about its people, and many of the stories he heard in the cottages are still current — though it is unlikely nowadays that small boys are dressed in petticoats to confuse the fairies who might otherwise kidnap them and put changelings in their place.

Hy-Brasil

In a world like this the vision of Hy-Brasil survives quite naturally, and in fact the lost Atlantis, which in Irish mythology is transmuted into the 'Land of the Young', was marked on many maps up to the development of advanced cartography in the last century. Given the right coincidence of light and cloud, plus the will to see visions, the mirage of the 'Isle of the Blessed' may still be observed from the Aran Islands, and indeed from points on the mainland coast as well. It has so much currency in Irish legend and poetry that, in such suitable conditions as the islands create, old beliefs become readily credible again.

County Mayo

Southern Peninsula

There are two roads from Leenane through the southern peninsula of Mayo, while a third backtracks for a short distance, then turns east to travel beneath the Tourmakeady Mountains along the western shore of Lough Mask to Partry.

Leenane to Westport

The two northern roads are endowed with glorious mountain scenery similar to that of Connemara, but growing wilder and more formidable as it travels further north. The direct route to Westport goes by Aasleagh Falls to defile along the Erriff Valley between the Sheefry Hills and the Partry Mountains, emerging then to cross a waste of

Connacht

moorland dominated by Ireland's holy mountain, Croagh Patrick. It is said that St Patrick prayed and fasted here for the forty days and nights of Lent, and a gruelling, barefoot pilgrimage to the summit still takes place in his honour on the last Sunday in July.

Ring Road to Louisburgh
The ring road, built to provide relief during the Famine, starts out along the northern arm of Killary, then turns inland through the valley of Delphi — no oracle here, but a thriving adventure centre offering equipment and instruction for the pursuit of a vast range of outdoor sports — to push through the mountains to Louisburgh.

Although a rash of uncouth new building disfigures the approach to Louisburgh, the combination of fine sea-angling facilities and magnificent sandy beaches remain irresistible to holiday-makers. The region is immensely rich in megalithic remains, and these along with details of local wildlife and ecology are thoroughly documented and illustrated in a delightful hand-drawn map available from tourist information offices. Below the headlands Clew Bay glitters with islands, most of them deserted but some bearing witness to previous habitation in the shape of evocative Early Christian ruins. A minor road from Louisburg leads out to Roonagh Quay where boats sail for the largest of the islands.

Clare Island
Lying in the mouth of the bay, Clare Island is a quiet place with a small population. In the past it was a fairly frenzied centre of activity, however, for this was the home of the redoubtable pirate queen, Grace O'Malley, who usurped her brother's claim to the lordship of the Western Isles and made life miserable and hazardous for everyone else in the area. She paid a visit to Queen Elizabeth in London in 1593, but accounts of their exchange differ markedly. Today the pirate queen lies buried in the grounds of the island's ancient ruined abbey, and in recent times her tower fortress has housed the more orthodox forces of coastguards and police.

Louisburg to Westport
The coast road from Louisburg turns east near the Old Head, where there is an example of prehistoric Atlantic oakwood, and runs on to the remainder of an important Augustinian foundation at Murrisk. Situated at the foot of Croagh Patrick, it was inevitable that the Abbey should be closely associated with Ireland's patron saint, and in former times it housed two cherished relics of his mission. St Patrick's Tooth and his famous Black Bell are now in the National Museum in Dublin, but the latter was displayed for the veneration of pilgrims in a shrine at the summit of the holy mountain until late in the last century. It was, they say, a present from an angel and was originally of silver. But the saint's struggle with local demons and/or his ferocious ringing of it to frighten the snakes away caused the Bell to corrode and turn

black. Small wonder.

Westport and Newport

Westport House

Near tiny Westport Harbour, where there are a number of excellent restaurants, stands one of the finest Georgian manor houses in Ireland. Open to visitors from spring to mid-autumn, Westport House is the seat of the Earls of Sligo and has been beautifully kept up, the present Lord Sligo showing much enterprise in establishing boutiques, a zoo and an art centre in the grounds. The house is approached by an impressive sweep of steps leading to an entrance hall with an ornate staircase of white marble. The rooms are notable for superb plaster-work by James Wyatt and contain an enviable collection of old Irish silver, family portraits and historical mementoes.

Westport Town

The town of Westport was designed late in the 18th century as an adjunct to Westport House, and it reflects a similar civilised spirit and pleasing perspectives. Its most dramatic feature is the Octagon with its Doric pillar at the centre, while down by the river canal tree-lined malls support some fine old Georgian houses. The Railway Hotel here has a good name, but the best value for money in the town is at Altamont House where Mrs Sheridan combines a first-class bed-and-breakfast operation with great personal warmth and friendliness.

The north road out of Westport goes past the turning for the town's championship golf course and the famous Glenans Sailing Centre, to run for about eight miles through pleasant country to the 17th-century village of Newport.

Newport House

There is another memorable Georgian house here. An earlier building than Westport, and smaller but no less elegantly proportioned, Newport House, which is now an hotel, is designed around a central, winding staircase with an exquisite lantern dome above it. As an hotel, it is acclaimed for its magnificent cellar, its fine kitchen and excellent private fishing grounds.

Coast Road to Ballina

From Newport the road runs west out to the seaside resort of Mulrany, then on around the mountainous Curraun Peninsula to the causeway connecting Achill Island with the mainland; the vegetation in this area is vivid with wild fuschia and rhododendron, fragrant with the scent of Mediterranean heather.

Achill Island

The eastern end of Achill is much favoured by boisterous holiday-

Connacht

makers in the summer, but further west there is magnificent cliff scenery, particularly at Minaun, and good roads for exploring the more remote villages of Keel, Dooagh and Dugort. Massive mountains rise behind the villages, and there was a thriving shark-fishing industry at Keem Bay. Off the tarred road, on the slopes of Slievemore, an ancient derelict village strikes at the heart with its desolation of small, roofless stone houses. But the tears are misplaced, for this was merely a 'booley' settlement providing temporary accommodation for cattle and the families of the herdsmen in summer long ago. The stone-built cottage and open turf fire of the Boley House restaurant at Keel gives an idea of how these temporary dwellings looked in their prime.

Bog of Erris; Blacksod Bay
There is really desolate country north of Clew Bay, however, and here the Famine struck hardest and lingers still in the memory of the scant population. The mountains stretch out to the vast Bog of Erris, where the gorse blazes for miles on end, and then the landscape breaks off in the bleak peninsula of Belmullet which supports no vegetation at all on its western coast. It is worth seeing the bare, uncomprising grandeur of Blacksod Bay, worth spending time in the area for the sake of excellent shooting and fishing.

Killala Bay
There is more cliff scenery along the northern coast road leading to Killala Bay, where a French force landed in a vain attempt to help the insurgents of 1798. Once again, the area is rich in megalithic monuments, as well as Early Christian remains, and there is rumour of a 3,000-year-old farmhouse recently discovered near the village of Ballycastle.

Ballina; Enniscoe House
Ballina, which is the biggest town in the county, is situated at the head of Killala Bay on the River Moy. Acknowledged as the most prolific salmon river in Ireland, the Moy attracts dedicated anglers by the score every year, many of them basing themselves at Mount Falcon Castle which maintains five private beats with gillies and boats for its guests. A road west from Ballina goes through Crossmolina to encircle Lough Conn, crossing the stream which connects the larger lake with Lough Cullen by a single-arched bridge at Pontoon. Enniscoe House is on its path.

Standing in wooded parkland with a private jetty on the lakeshore, this fine Georgian family house boasts another example of the lantern dome so notable at Newport. The 300-acre estate is run as a working farm and the house provides comfortable accommodation for visitors with four-poster or canopy bedsteads in the main bedrooms. The local historical society is developing a 'heritage centre' for North County Mayo in a yard behind the house.

South Mayo

Knock

The county capital, Castlebar, lies south of Lough Conn, and south-east of it stands the village of Knock which was apparently the scene of a divine apparition nearly a century ago and is still a place of pilgrimage. A new airport here gives direct access to the West of Ireland, and is well served by regular Ryanair flights from Manchester, Birmingham and Liverpool, as well as London's Gatwick and Luton airports.

Ballintubber Abbey

The principal town in south Mayo is Ballinrobe, which made local history for a few splendid years by staging a small and enterprising opera festival in the parish hall; alas, the festival is now defunct and its talented organiser fled to more fertile artistic conditions across the Channel. The town remains, however, and its situation on the eastern shore of Lough Mask makes it a good base for excursions to restored 13th century Ballintubber Abbey, which has survived as a place of worship for some 700 years. The restoration of this fine Augustinian foundation uncovered the papal seal bestowed on it in 1463 by Pope Pius II, and also brought to light some of the earlier cloister arcade and a hospice for pilgrims. The Chapter House has a striking west doorway with pointed arch, while within the Abbey a well-preserved Renaissance tomb recalls a scion of the O'Malley family.

Moore Hall; Cong Abbey

To the south lies the burned shell of Moore Hall, which was the home of the Irish writer, George Moore, and below this, on a wooded isthmus between Lough Mask and Lough Corrib, the tiny village of Cong with its two famous and monumental buildings. The imposing pile of Ashford Castle was built as a home for a member of the Guinness family in the 19th century, but later passed into commercial hands and became an hotel. The grounds are beautifully laid out, and outside the demesne stand the restored remains of the Augustinian Abbey of Cong. There is a 14th-century stone cross in the village of Cong, but the great jewelled processional Cross of Cong rests in the National Museum of Dublin — despite a spirited attempt by a local priest some years back to seize it and restore it to its traditional home.

Lough Mask House; Moytura Plain

Near Cong, on the Ballinrobe road, stands Lough Mask House, once the home of Captain Boycott whose treatment at the hands of his tenants gave the English language a new verb. Oscar Wilde's father had a house in this neighbourhood, too, and profited by the megaliths of the area to devise theories which are regarded as fanciful by present-day archaeologists. There was plenty of material for Sir William's imagination to work on, for between Cong and the village of Neale (pronounced 'Nail') lies the Plain of Moytura where in prehistoric times the *Tuath Dé Danann* inflicted their first serious defeat on the Firbolgs. A second and decisive victory came seven years later at the Battle of Northern Moytura near Sligo and the poor Firbolgs were vanquished for ever.

County Sligo

A strange, introverted landscape of purple and greens and grey, County Sligo holds such a concentration of antiquities that it might be considered one of the oldest parts of the world — and also one of the youngest, for Lake Achree in the north of the county is said to have been formed by a volcano as late as 1490.

The whole area is vivid with myth and legend, with history and fairytale, and it is often difficult to disentangle one from the other — which hardly matters to anyone but a professional historian. For the rest of us there is no harm, and indeed considerable passing pleasure, in going along as easily with the story of Queen Maeve buried beneath the huge cairn of Knocknarea as with the authentic account of Red Hugh O'Donnell's victory at the 'Battle of the Curlews' in 1599.

Inniscrone to Sligo Town

The coast of Sligo has long, sandy beaches on the Atlantic, and fact and fiction begin to merge around the sheltered seaside resort of Inniscrone where a group of boulders has been identified as the children of a mermaid. The boulders are a tangible fact, and it would be as hard to disprove as to prove the old story that their mother transformed her children so cruelly as she escaped her human husband and slipped back into the sea.

The MacFirbis Family

No easier to discover the whole truth about the MacFirbis family whose stronghold stood a few miles away. For while their alleged descent from the *Tuatha De Danann* may be disputed, they have a firm claim on history in the surviving evidence of some three centuries' activity as scribes. The 'Yellow Book of Leacan', compiled c. 1391, is in Trinity College, Dublin; the 'Great Book of Leacan', which dates from the follwing century, is in the Royal Irish Academy, and 'The Book of Genealogies of Ireland', which was not completed until the seond half of the 17th century, is in University College, Dublin. The family were cartographers, too, and it is interesting to compare a 17th-century MacFirbis plan of a ring-fort and souterrain at Rathmulcah with the present day reality. Of the nine chambers shown on the ancient plan, the earthen rampart now allows access to only five.

Easkey to Ballisodare

At Easkey a vertical fissure in an Ice Age builder is attributed to a sword thrust by the mighty legendary hero, Fionn Mac Cumhail, and there are several forts and a large dolmen in the vicinity to provide materal for other ancient stories. More recent history is represented by a ruined castle once occupied by the O'Dowd family, and then the road travels in line with the coast through Dromore West and Skreen, turning south to follow a deep inlet to Ballisodare and the remains of a 7th-century monastery with later Romanesque door.

Knocknarea
To the north rises the chopped-off cone of Knocknarea, not much more than 1,000 feet high but dominating the surrounding countryside with that dramatic silhouette so characteristic of many mountains in Sligo. The immense cairn on the summit is believed to conceal a Bronze Age tomb, though it is more popularly said to be the grave of that mischievous Queen Maeve whose lawless pursuit of the Brown Bull of Cooley caused such strife and bloodshed on the other side of the country. The story goes that the wicked queen at last received her come-uppance through the agency of a crosscountry slingshot launched by the King of Ulster to avenge Cuchulainn. There is not much chance of checking its accuracy, however, for whatever remains lie on the top of Knockerea are formidably protected by some 40,000 tons of loose chippings.

Knocknarea falls away in grim screes and precipices, with the close, tree-choked chasm of Knocknarea Glen below leading west to Carrowmore. This is one of the biggest megalithic cemeteries in Europe, and although much despoiled by time and scavengers, still contains a remarkable number of antiquities. It is said to be the graveyard of those killed in the second Battle of Moytura; but this is all past history now, if history it ever was, and probably of little interest to the people who choose the nearby village of Strandhill for a seaside holiday.

Strandhill
Open to the Atlantic, Strandhill is a popular centre for wind-surfing and is often chosen for international competitions. But around the corner, in the shelter of a curving spit of coastline, is the gentler beach of Culleenamore, and less than two miles away the fleshpots of Knockmuldowney House. This fine Georgian country estate possesses a restaurant that has attracted the favourable attention of Michelin, and is noted for the fresh food gathered from its own grounds and neighbouring farms. It provides first-class accommodation, and at IR£12.50 for dinner is uncommonly reasonable in price. Sligo's little airport is within easy reach, and across the bay at Rosses Point there is an eighteen-hole championship golf course.

Sligo Town
Most of the county town of Sligo was built within the past hundred

and fifty years, including the Yeats Memorial Centre, which houses the Yeats Summer School and also an English language school for children. But there is the splendid inspiration of the 18th century beneath 19th-century alterations in St John's Church, which was designed by Cassels in 1730.

Dominican Abbey

Inspiring too are the ruins of the great Dominican abbey now undergoing major conservation treatment, one of the glories of Irish mediaeval architecture. Destroyed by fire in 1414, it was immediately re-built in the style of the time, though the eight lancet windows on the south side of the choir are from the original 13th-century edifice. The rood-screen, which separated the choir from the nave, has been partly reconstructed, and the carved high altar is the only one of its kind still in place in any monastic ruin in Ireland.

Yeats Country

Sligo is a comfortable town, and a convenient base for exploring the Yeats Country. Lough Gill is on its doorstep, and may be explored by boat, stopping at the lake island of Inishfree which inspired one of Yeats's best-known poems. On the southern shore of the lough stands 'Dooney's Rock', another source of inspiration for Yeats.

Magheraghanrush Cairn

Overlooking the tranquil lake and woodland scene is the splendid court cairn of Magheraghanrush. The tomb has a fifty-foot oval central court with two other burial chambers opening off it, while in a field lower down there is a wedge-shaped gallery grave, a fort with a souterrain (or underground stone passage) and a stone circle. The contrast between the gentle features of the lake scenery and the stern man-made megaliths on the hill above is thought-provoking.

Yeats's Grave

All this country north of Sligo is closely associated with Yeats, who spent so much time there and brought so many of its legends into his poetry — or perhaps invented them himself. The road runs out through Rosses Point to Drumcliff where the poet is buried. His grave with his own epitaph carved on the headstone — 'Cast a cold eye on life, on death. Horseman, pass by!' — lies in the shadow of 'bare Ben Bulben's Head', another stark mountain sacred to the romantic memory of Diarmuid and Gráinne.

Local Legends

Their story bears strong resemblance to the Tristan legend, though it parts company towards the end when Classical myth is invoked by a vulnerable heel. For Diarmuid ran off with the King's betrothed whom he had been sent to escort to her marriage, and they wandered over Ireland together until the King, who was no other than Fionn

Mac Cumhail and therefore in the order of things bound to win, sent a message to say that he had accepted the situation. To celebrate his reconciliation with the lovers Fionn invited Diarmuid to hunt a black boar — which in some versions of the tale was Diarmuid's own half-brother magically transformed, or maybe the King's. At the end of it all, one of the boar's bristles pierced Diarmuid's foot, which was his only vulnerable spot, and he died. Gráinne, being a practical woman, married the King.

Believe this or not as one will, it is more difficult to refute the story of the 'Battle of the Books', which resulted in St Columba setting off for Iona to convert the heathen. The Book in question was a psalter belonging to St Finian or St Finbarr of which St Columba made a secret copy: St Finian demanded the copy, St Columba refused, on the principle of 'to every cow its calf' the King declared for the former saint and a mighty battle in which 3,000 men were killed took place at Cuildrevine. St Columba won, but quite properly overcome by remorse at the carnage he had caused, repented his ways, built a monastery at Drumcliff near the site of the battle and then sailed off on his evangelising mission.

The only strange factor about this story is that some or all of it may be true. For the book, known as the *cathac,* exists: it came into the hands of the O'Donnell clans, who employed it as a talisman in battle, and then at last found its way to the Royal Irish Academy in Dublin where it rests today.

North to Grange; Inishmurray
East of Drumcliff in the Dartry mountains, lies Glencar with the rushing waterfalls that Yeats loved. But the main road continues north to Grange and along the coast to Cliffoney and Mullaghmore. Inland lie the great megalithic tombs of Creevykeel, while at Grange boats may be hired to go out to Inishmurray — and even in a country so well endowed with ruins as Ireland, it is worth visiting the ruins of this monastic settlement founded by St Molaise at the beginning of the 6th century. The monastery remains are surrounded by an immensely thick wall, some thirteen feet high, and inside the enclosure are the ruins of the ancient churches, *clochans,* a sweat-house and altars — one of the last incorporating 'cursing stones'. Outside there is a little oratory known as the 'Church of the Women', and until the island was abandoned in 1947 it was the custom to bury women outside the monastery walls and men within.

Ardternon Castle
South of Grange a small peninsula pushes out to culminate in Raghly and the ruins of 17th-century Ardternon Castle which was the former seat of the Gore family. It is, in fact, a semi-fortified manor house with two circular towers flanking the entrance, a semi-circular stair-projection at the rear, and a bawn wall enclosing a courtyard.

Connacht

Excavations have begun here prior to a thorough restoration.

Lissadell
Lissadell, where the Gore-Booth family lives now, is on the same road and is open to the public. This lovely late Georgian manor has been sadly impoverished in recent years, apparently due to repressive litigation by the Irish Land Commission, and is now a forlorn but still beautiful echo of the house Yeats described, with its 'great windows open to the south'. Here Countess Markievicz was born, grew up and went on to fight with the Irish Citizens Army in 1916, and two years later to become the first woman elected to Parliament at Westminster. She refused to take her seat, but was part of the first *Dáil Eireann* in Dublin.

Southern County Sligo

Ballymote
The ancient town of Ballymote is a good base for exploring south County Sligo and the country around Lough Arrow. In the town itself there are substantial mediaeval remains and the vast 14th-century de Burgo castle with its six towers should not be missed, nor the old Franciscan friary where the 'Book of Ballymote' was compiled. This code gives the key to the linear script known as *ogham*, which is incised on so many standing stones of the 4th and 5th centuries.

Carrowkeel and Kesh
Prehistory takes over again at Carrowkeel, on a hilltop in the Brickleive Mountains, where there is another impressive collection of passage graves. Excavations on this site revealed pottery, bone pins and stone hammer pendants dating from late in the Stone Age. At Kesh the bones of Arctic lemming, reindeer, bears and wolves were discovered in caves in the western hill faces. The unhappy Diarmuid was said to have had his home here while another classical legend is echoed in the story that the High King, Cormac Mac Art, was nurtured in one of the caves by a she-wolf.

Prehistoric Sites
More than two hundred lake dwellings, or *crannógs*, which were inhabited between 1000 BC and 1000 AD, have been identified amongst the islands of Lough Gara, while on the other side of the county, beyond the excellent shooting grounds of Tubbercurry, a pre-bog enclosure, complete with house and cultivation ridges, has been found in recent years at Bonniconlon.

Round Lough Arrow to Lough Nasool
From the southern shore of Lough Arrow there is a pleasant drive with yet again plenty of remains from the past in the vicinity. Ballinafad Castle, defending a pass across the Curlew Hills, dates from the 16th century, Ballindoon Friary from earlier in the same era, and

Castlebaldwin from the 17th century. There is a good place to stop at Coopershill near Riverstown, where a fine Georgian mansion has been converted into award-winning restaurant and comfortable guest house. The River Arrow flows through its grounds, and there are trout and coarse fish in local waters.

Coopershill House was completed in 1774 and its history is well authenticated. But just a few miles away legend comes into its own once more at Lough Nasool, the 'Lake of the Eye', which disappears through a hole in its bed from time to time. The eye in question belonged, and perhaps still does, to Balor, who was a giant and one of the nastiest characters in Irish mythology. His activities, always malevolent, were largely confined to his home on Tory Island off the Donegal coast, but there were occasional frightful forays to the mainland, and for all anyone knows to the contrary, Balor still keeps watch through his baleful 'eye' at the bottom of Lough Nasool.

The counties of Leitrim and Roscommon lie in the eastern region of Connacht and have more to do with the River Shannon and its lakes. They are described in Chapter V of this book.

Crawfordsburn Inn, Co. Down

Ulster Province

For centuries the nine counties of Ulster constituted a powerful and independent realm where even the Norman invasion made little headway. The O'Neills of Tyrone and the O'Donnells of Tyrconnell successfully fought off most military expeditions sent against the north and, although they accepted earldoms from Queen Elizabeth, continued to rule according to ancient Gaelic tradition within their territories.

Towards the end of the 16th century the northern chieftains were holding their own, but pressures from outside were increasing and they sought help from the Continent. A Spanish army landed at Kinsale in the south of the country in 1601, and O'Neill and O'Donnell marched to meet them. This was probably their principal mistake, for outside their own territory they were on unfamiliar ground and no longer invincible; however, they were in fit fighting form when they reached Kinsale and settled down to besiege the English forces which were already besieging the Spaniards in the town. Had the siege continued, there was still a chance of success for the Irish, but they were beaten in open battle and forced to submit while still strong enough to obtain honourable terms: although they retained their lands, their independence had been broken and, sensing worse to come, the Earls of Ulster sailed away into voluntary exile six years later.

The Crown lost no time in expropriating the northern territories and the great Plantation of Ulster began. The new settlers were mostly Scots, good farmers and craftsmen who built neat towns and gave the northern countryside much of the character it has today: it is generally of a tidier and more orderly nature than the country further south, and in recent years the National Trust for Northern Ireland has done much to preserve this heritage. The Treaty of 1921, however, altered the boundaries of Ulster once again, leaving Donegal, Cavan and Monaghan in the Republic, while Antrim, Down, Armagh, Tyrone, Fermanagh and Derry form the United Kingdom province of Northern Ireland. The three southern counties of the old province of Ulster — Fermanagh, Cavan and Monaghan — are part of the lakelands of Ireland and are described in Chapter V of this book.

Belfast and County Antrim

Belfast

Belfast is one of the youngest capital cities in the world, and its development over the past three centuries represents some of the fastest growth in history.

It was originally the site of a fort on the River Lagan. The Normans built a castle there in 1177; Edward Bruce destroyed it in 1316, and for the next 300 years Belfast remained a bone of contention between Irish and English. It was of small account, however, and in 1657 the population was hardly more than 500. Within thirty years it had quadrupled: the Scottish immigrants who arrived with the Plantation began building ships and manufacturing linen, and by 1800 the population had grown to 20,000. It was approaching 300,000 when Belfast acquired the formal status of a city towards the end of the last century, and is now in the region of half a million.

It had all been done by industry: by a determination to build and prosper, a will to work and work hard, a thrifty development of business resources, plus the encouraging context created by the general industrial expansion of the 19th century. The evidence of this golden age stands still in the great Victorian buildings that are Belfast's pride and their façades are often decorated with sculptures symbolising the principles that animate the city's life.

City Hall

The heart of the city is Donegall Square, which is dominated by the Renaissance-style bulk of the City Hall. This massive building with four corner towers and a 175-foot copper dome has an interior lavishly

decorated with marble and a large mural of Belfast's industrial history.
A fine sculpture commemorates those who lost their lives in the *Titanic*
disaster, for the ship had been built in Belfast's yards.

Chief Buildings
Two bastions of education, the College of Technology and the Royal
Belfast Academical Institution, stand near one another in the centre
of the city and, opposite the Institute, the Presbyterian General
Assembly building contains some striking examples of Irish stained
glass and has a handsome pinnacled clock tower. The market area is
dominated by the massive building of the Royal Courts of Justice.
The Custom House in mellow, golden-coloured stone is one of the
best buildings in the city, and beside it stands the Albert Memorial,
another clock tower, Gothic in style and leaning slightly to one side.

Churches
A few yards away St George's Church presents a handsome classical
portico, while after some seventy years work St Anne's Cathedral is
at last completed. The basic design is Hiberno-Romanesque and the
roof of the baptistry is a mosaic of some 150,000 pieces of glass
representing the Creation. The three entrance doorways of the west
front have recessed arches and tympanal sculptures, while the nave,
which is eighty-five feet wide, is paved with Irish marble and Canadian
maple. The pillars of the arcades that separate it from the aisles have
carved capitals and above them corbels bearing sculptured heads
commemorating various dignitaries of the Church of Ireland.

St Patrick's Church, which houses a 15th-century metal reliquary
known as the 'Shrine of St Patrick's Hand', has a chapel decorated
by Sir John Lavery, and there is a fine fan-vaulted ceiling in St
Malachy's Church. The oldest church in Belfast, however, is towards
the outskirts of the city at Knockbreda. It was built in 1737 and is the
work of Richard Cassels who was responsible for so much distinguished Georgian architecture in Ireland.

Museum; University
The Ulster Museum and Art Gallery are agreeably situated in the
Botanic Gardens, all three worth a leisurely visit. In addition to Irish
antiquities, the Museum has a special section devoted to the treasure
recovered only some twenty years ago from the Spanish galleas,
Girona, which sank off the Giant's Causeway during the dispersal of
the Armada in 1588. Queen's University is also in this neighbourhood,
though the original 19th-century Tudor-Gothic building, which is often
compared to Magdalen College at Oxford, is now only the nucleus of
a vast modern development. This area is the liveliest social centre in
Belfast with plenty of restaurants, pubs and cafés doing thriving
business in the evenings and at lunchtime.

Music; Arts Festival
The 19th-century, which saw the rapid expansion of Belfast as an

industrial force, promoted the development of cultural activity at the same time. This is reflected in the high standard of the Ulster Orchestra, and in the Belfast Opera House which is a glorious late-Victorian extravaganza, situated conveniently for the inner man on the same street as one of the city's most popular restaurants, *La Belle Epoque*. The opera season takes place during the second half of September, but the peak of the cultural year comes in November with the Belfast Arts Festival, organised by the university and said to be second only to Edinburgh.

Ulster is uncommonly well provided with brass bands, flute bands, silver bands — all sorts of bands, and these come into their own when the great sectarian parades take place in the summer, July 12th for the Orangemen and August 15th for the Hibernians. They can be spectacular and impressive, but perhaps best watched from a safe distance by those with no stake in local politics.

Belfast Port
The port of Belfast is a lively and exciting place, with seven miles of quay approached by a deep-water channel. A vast volume of trade is handled at the huge docks, and their equipment includes some of the largest cranes in the world. The city's great ship-building industry is centred here, and many of the world's famous liners were launched from Belfast yards.

Parks; Castle Stormont
Despite its industrial concentration, Belfast does not go short of open green space: there are about ten public parks scattered around the city and its suburbs, while behind it a chain of hills curves in from the west. Cave Hill, which is only four miles from the city centre, is said to resemble Napoleon's profile and has some formidable crags and steep ascents. On the slopes are the gardens of Hazelwood and Bellevue — the latter including the zoo — and there is a striking example of 19th-century Gothic in Belfast Castle. This baronial pile with its six-storey tower and Baroque staircase was presented to the city by Lord Shaftesbury in 1934 and is now being restored. Higher up there is a chain of neolithic caves, and a splendid view over the surrounding country extending as far as the monumental white parliamentary buildings of Stormont on their hilltop site.

Belfast Lough
Shaw's Bridge; Ballylesson
On the other side of Belfast Lough there is a pleasant walk along a towpath by the River Lagan to Shaw's Bridge, so named for John Shaw Brown who established the famous 'Shamrock Damask' linen mills at Edenderry. At Ballylesson there is an earthen fort with a dolmen in the centre, while at Fort Hill more ancient earthworks command a fine view of Belfast city.

Ulster

Holywood
Travelling into County Down along the southern shore of the lough, the town of Holywood is remarkable for a 70-ft. mast with a weather-vane on top. It is known locally as the 'maypole' and is the successor of many that have stood on the spot since 1700 when a Dutch ship went aground on the eve of May Day. Holywood is considered commuter country by Belfast people, and has an excellent restaurant called *The Schooner* which specialises in duck served with figs. Nearby, on the main road, there is another example of Scottish-baronial architecture in the former archepiscopal palace which has been transformed into Culloden Hotel.

Cultra
A little further on, at Cultra, the Ulster Folk and Transport Museum illustrates the history of the countryside in a magnificent assembly of reconstructed farmhouses, cottages and work buildings. It has taken some thirty years to dismantle these buildings on their native sites, transport and re-build them stone-by-stone at Cultra, but the result is well worth it. There are two principal sections, and demonstrations of traditional farming go on throughout the year in the rural area. The other section is devoted to urban housing, and already a village has been assembled which includes early 19th-century terraces taken from the streets of Belfast, and a rectory dating from 1717 which has been transplanted from Toombridge. Exhibits at the Transport Museum include a three-masted schooner, a model of an historic monoplane and the prototype of the first vertical take-off jet aircraft, which was developed by Short Brothers of Belfast.

Lough Neagh Area

The Lough
Much of the western boundary of County Antrim is formed by the shoreline of Lough Neagh. With an area of 150 square miles, this is the biggest lake in Ireland and Britain, and also Europe's greatest supply source of eels. Legend has it that Fionn MacCumhail created the Lough by scooping up a great clod of earth and tossing it out into the Irish Sea, where it instantly became the Isle of Man. Science attributes its formation to glacial action some 20,000 years ago. The horse-god, Eochu, lord of the underworld, is said to live beneath the waters which, perhaps due to his influence, are reputed to have the power of petrifying wood. In fact 'Lough Neagh hones' are created over many years by the gradual action of silica salts on wood fibre.

River Bann
Eight rivers flow into Lough Neagh, but only the Bann flows out again. Bird and plant life flourishes along the flat, sedgy shoreline and on the half-dozen small, uninhabited islands, while old-fashioned customs survive for a long time in the small, thatched villages along the shore. There are quaint curiosities in the neighbourhood, such as the 'Willow

Pattern Garden' at Aghagallon: this is a gardener's folly of arches and towers and strange stones and fossils now sadly neglected.

Antrim
The ancient county town of Antrim is the most important and biggest population centre in the vicinity of the lake. Picturesquely situated where Six Mile Water enters Lough Neagh, it was founded as a monastic settlement in Early Christian times and has one of the finest Round Towers in the country. More than 90 feet high, it has a cross-carved stone over the lintel and a great hollowed boulder at its base. The door is nearly 10 feet above the ground.

The early 18th-century courthouse in the Market Square of Antrim is one of the best buildings in the town and still serves its original purpose. Opposite is the entrance to Antrim Castle, which was built in 1662 and survived into the 20th century until the troubles of 1922. The estate gardens were laid out by Le Notre, the distinguished landscape gardener of Versailles, and are designed on a grand scale. They include ornamental ponds flanked by hedges, a stone bridge over the river and a Norman motte with a spiral pathway. The 19th-century stables and coach house in the grounds have been converted into an arts centre with an open-air theatre in the courtyard.

Randalstown to Crumlin
At Randalstown the wooded demesne of Shane's Castle stretches down to the lakeside where a narrow-gauge railway runs along the shore. The headquarters of the Railway Preservation Society of Ireland is situated not far away in the little holiday resort of Whitehead, and from here a famous old steam express train known as the 'Portrush Flyer' puffs off on excursions during the season.

All this region is within easy touring reach of Belfast Airport, and there is plenty to see, from early times to recent.

At Bog Head near the county town there is a two-storey souterrain which is the only one of its kind in Ireland; an ancient rath, or earthwork, at Rathmore Trench is believed to have been the seat of the Dalriada kings in the 6th century. At Crumlin near the centre of the eastern lakeshore, there is a wooded glen with a small river tumbling through a series of cascades, and in the glen a folly, part house, part cave, with Gothic entrance arches, which is said to have been built for a Muslim.

Routes to Belfast
There are three feasible routes from the lake country back to Belfast. The most direct is from Crumlin via Nutts Corner, but there is more interest to the north where the motorway from Randalstown passes by Templepatrick. This is one of the oldest Protestant settlements in Ireland, and in Upton House presents a mixture of architectural styles

dating mainly from the beginning of the 17th century but flanked by Norman towers. The house stands on the site of the 13th-century priory of the Knights Hospitaller of St John who sailed with Prince Edward on the last Crusade.

The prettiest route back from Lough Neagh is through the exceptionally lovely country that stretches south from Glenavy to join the motorway at Lisburn. Situated on the Lagan river, Lisburn has fine 18th-century assembly rooms which now house an exhibition devoted to the linen industry of which the town was the centre, and only a mile away the village of Lambeg recalls the origin of the famous Orange drums. It is worth a short detour south to visit Hillsborough with its Georgian town houses and market; its splendid castle, which was formerly the residence of the Governor of Northern Ireland, and, best of all, the well-preserved 17th-century fort built by the Colonel Arthur Hill who gave the town its name.

Antrim Coast

The Antrim coast is one of the most remarkable stretches of country in the world. Its geological composition goes back something like 300 million years to the formation of the earth's crust, and includes the biggest lava fields in these islands, trias resulting from the sands of a once-torrid desert; at one point no less than sixteen different strata are visible in the cliffs. Behind lies a celebrated wilderness of hills and glens, heavily endowed with legends and fairytales — and also noted for the manufacture of *poteen*. This illicit spirit, which is distilled with equal enthusiasm in remote parts of the west and south-west of Ireland, is sometimes based on potatoes, sometimes on grain; it has a fiery potency which augurs caution in its consumption and heavy fines for those caught making it.

Carrickfergus

The road to the coast runs out along the northern shore of Belfast Lough, coming first to Carrickfergus which has the best mediaeval castle in the country. The town takes its name from Fergus MacErc who was once king of Dalriada and established a colony in Scotland, taking with him, it is said, the Stone of Scone which is now in Westminster Abbey. The castle, however, was built by the Normans about 1180. Edward Bruce took it early in the 14th century and in the succeeding years it suffered the usual attacks by warring factions; it remains however in an exceptionally good state of preservation with even its ancient portcullis still intact.

The parish church off the market place was built about the same time as the castle, but underwent considerable restoration early in the 17th century. There is an inn dating from the same period in the High Street, while both town hall and market house are Georgian. There are mediaeval banquets in the castle during June, and in July the old Quarterly Irish feast of *Lughnasa* is celebrated with a great two-day costume fair and crafts market.

Islandmagee
The road goes on to Whitehead, then branches off in a spur along the narrow peninsula of Islandmagee. Strange basalt cliffs and boulders provide a suitable setting for the witchcraft that was practised here until the 18th century; the trial and sentencing of several women in 1711 put a stop to it, though in the early 1960s the discovery of some black cloaks and candles in a cave suggested that old habits might after all still prevail.

Larne
From Whitehead the main road travels north to Larne, where the car ferries come in from Scotland after a mere seventy-minute sea journey. A dangerous group of rocks out at sea is known as the 'Maidens', and at the entrance to the harbour a replica of a Round Tower does duty as a lighthouse. A 16th-century castle ruin dominates the curving promontory known as the 'Curran', where an immense quantity of Stone Age artefacts has been discovered.

Larne to Glenarm
The coast road leaves Larne through Black Cave Tunnel, emerging above a whirling sea gully known as the 'Devil's Churn'. From here it runs close to the coast through superb scenery, by a wild, natural amphitheatre of crags, to the basalt cliffs of Ballygalley Head and its ruined castle. Beyond lies White Bay with thousands of tiny fossils deposited by the sea in prehistoric times, and then the pretty village of Glenarm. The glen stretches back into the hinterland, while behind the village Glenarm Castle is still the property of the Earls of Antrim, whose ancestor, Sorley Boy MacDonnell, was almost as severe a threat to Queen Elizabeth as the great Earl of Tyrone. Built in the 17th century, the castle strongly resembles the Tower of London but has several later additions in Gothic, Tudor and Jacobean styles. A raised beach north of Glenarm has yielded another hoard of Stone Age implements, and near here the 'slipping village' of Straidkilly has been partly abandoned as the upper chalk stratum of its foundations moves gradually downhill over the seaward-tilted lias.

Carnlough
Carnlough is a sandy crescent bay at the mouth of the shallowest of the Glens of Antrim. The mountains sweep towards the sea in steep escarpments to form Garron Point, where great landslides of rock combine with lias clays to form clearly-marked shelves of basalt and limestone. Facing out to sea is the strange chalk water-sculpture called the 'White Lady', while on a natural shelf above stands the tower which the Marchioness of Londonderry built to provide employment during the Famine.

Ulster

In their time, the worked-out quarries above the little resort provided ample building material for Carnlough. The bridge and the clock tower and the old courthouse are all built of great squared blocks of the local limestone, and it had its place, too, in the embellishment of the picturesque small harbour which is a popular port of call for yachtsmen. Nearby stands the *Londonderry Arms*, which is one of the nicest hotels in the whole of Ireland. Once the property of Winston Churchill, it has been in the hands of the O'Neill family for many years now and is a spacious comfortable establishment with fine furnishings and a first-class restaurant that has won several awards for its food.

Red Bay, Glenariff
Beyond the Point the sandstone cliffs of Red Bay form a chain deeply scored by caves such as that which housed Ann Murray, a celebrated *poteen*-maker of the last century, and, in the 18th century, a school. Beyond the village of Waterfoot an arch cut through the sandstone leads to a ruined castle of the MacDonnells, while further on Glenariff, which is the most famous of the Antrim Glens, emerges from between steep mountainsides.

Glens of Antrim
To the north, three glens converge at the village of Cushendall where a gentle river wanders past a golf course to the sea. There are lively, old-fashioned pubs here, and a small, friendly hotel called the 'Thornlea' which serves immense breakfasts-in-bed on request. Above the village a megalithic tomb and stone circle on the slopes of Mount Tievebulliagh are said to mark the grave of the poet, Ossian, while further up the mountain the site of a Stone Age axe factory has been identified.

Cushendun to Tor Head
At Cushendun there is a quaint example of model-village architecture by Clough Williams-Ellis, who built the terrace of white-washed houses in the square early this century. From here the main road cuts inland by Ballypatrick Forest and the little lake of Loughnareena, which sometimes floods the roads, at others runs completely dry. The coast road however goes out through Culraney to Torr Head which is only thirteen miles distant from Scotland.

Murlough Bay; Rathlin Island
Beyond lies Murlough Bay with the schists which are the original surface formed by the earth's cooling. Sixteen different rock strata are visible in the 600-foot cliffs of Fair Head, and from here there is a spendid view of Rathlin Island. Its white cliffs are raucous with the cries of seabirds, and in the base of the cliffs is the cave where Robert Bruce sought refuge and learned his famous lesson from the spider.

Rathlin was hotly disputed by Scots and Irish in times past, and the decisive factor in the lawsuit which awarded the islands to the Irish was the absence of snakes. These, it has always been claimed, were driven out of Ireland by St Patrick, though there are those who contend that the saint was thinking of the druids when he spoke of reptiles. During his wars with the English, Sorley Boy MacDonnell sent his family and most of the local women and old people to Rathlin for safety, but they were followed by the English who massacred the lot. Thirty families still live on the island, which may be visited by boat from Ballycastle.

Ballycastle
Ballycastle is a seaside resort and market town beneath the isolated summit of Knocklayd mountain; Glenshesk and Glentaisie meet at its bay, and the area is rich in mediaeval remains. Here in 1898 Marconi experimented with his wireless telegraph, and here in earlier times legend says that Deirdre of the Sorrows with her lover and his brothers landed on their mistaken return from Scotland. Ballycastle also lays claim to be the place where their wicked stepmother changed the Children of Lír into swans which swam about disconsolately until the sound of the first Christian bell restored them to human shape. Other parts of Ireland claim this celebrated incident as well.

Portbradden to Kinbane Castle
The smallest church in Ireland, measuring a mere twelve feet by six-and-a-half, may be inspected at Portbradden, while from the pretty little limestone harbour set amongst the rocks at Ballintoy, boats set out for excursions to Sheep Island and its colony of cormorants. One of the most daunting tourist attractions in the district is the rope bridge which sways about eighty feet above boiling seas to give access to the salmon fishery on the rock island of Carrick-a-rede. Not for the timorous. The country is subject to severe erosion in this area, and there is an exciting boat trip to be made through the cave that penetrates the promontory beneath the ruined 16th-century gatehouse of Kinbane Castle.

Giant's Causeway
To the west, beyond the fragmentary remains of Dunseverick Castle at Benbane Head, lies the Giant's Causeway. This extraordinary complex of basalt columns marching out into the sea was once thought to be a path built by giants across the water to Scotland. More prosaic scientific explanation has since prevailed, but the great spectacle remains breathtaking in its primeval splendour. No amount of quaint naming of the strange formations can rob the Causeway of its grandeur, and although it may be inspected cursorily from the coast, the only way to see it properly is on foot. It is worth while attending a showing of the excellent explanatory film at the local Visitor Centre before deciding between a two-mile walk and a fairly comprehensive five-mile circuit that takes in the Grand, Middle and Little Causeways, as well as Lacada Point where the treasure of the

Girona was recovered in 1968.

Dunluce Castle
Further west along the coast, the landscape is dominated by the vast ruins of Dunluce Castle. This stark and dramatic mass stands on an isolated rock crag, and a wooden bridge replaces the drawbridge which was once the only landward access to the castle; in the rock beneath there is a large cave which served as a secret entrance from the sea. Dunluce came to an end one stormy night in 1639 when, as the household was preparing for a dinner party, part of the cliff collapsed and took most of the kitchens, including the staff, into the sea with it. After this the Earls of Antrim removed themselves first to Ballymagarry House a few miles away and then to Glenarm Castle.

Portrush; Bushmills
West of Dunluce a range of chalk cliffs with many caves and strange formations leads to Portrush. The fine beaches on each side of this little peninsula make it a popular holiday resort, and from here it is possible to cross over into Derry or else work back inland to Bushmills where the oldest whiskey distillery in the world opens its doors regularly to visitors. There is a Michelin-starred restaurant in the area, and at the recently renovated *Bushmills Inn* residents may enjoy orange juice freshly squeezed while they wait at breakfast-time, plus some of the best coffee the country has to offer.

Ballymoney; Ballymena
There are some nice late Georgian houses to the south in Ballymoney, and several interesting churches. About seven miles away at Dervock lived the ancestors of the American president, William McKinley, who was assassinated around the turn of the century. At Kilraughts, in a bog to the east of Ballymoney, four Bronze Age trumpets were discovered early in the 19th-century, and proved to be still in working order after some 2,500 years. Further south again, the town of Ballymena claims St Patrick as its most distinguished emigrant, for it was near here on Slemish mountain that he worked as a slave during his early captivity in Ireland.

County Down

With its fertile countryside and gentle, cultivated hills, County Down is one of the best farming counties in Ireland. The granite range of the Mourne Mountains rises to the south, while along the eastern boundary rich agricultural land is watered by the River Bann. The whole area is rich in ancient ecclesiastical traditions.

Co. Down Coast

Bangor; Donaghadee
The road which runs out through Holywood along the southern shore

of Belfast Lough comes to the first important religious site at Bangor. Pleasantly situated on the coast, Bangor today has only a few mediaeval fragments surviving from the monastic settlement that was established there in the 7th-century, but the great 'Bangor Antiphony', which was compiled in those early days, survives and is now in the Ambrosian Library at Milan.

Today Bangor is Northern Ireland's biggest seaside resort, while a few miles further along the coast Donaghadee forms another popular but smaller holiday centre. Here there is a 19th-century castle built on an old Norman motte, some good Georgian houses and a pub which it is said was visited by Peter the Great during his grand tour in 1697: 'Of all beverages' said the Czar, who was no mean judge, 'the Irish is the best.'

Ards Peninsula

Off the coast lie the deserted Copeland Islands, which may be visited by boat from Donaghadee, while a scenic route continues down along the Ards Peninsula. Protecting Stranford Lough and its dozens of islands from the open sea, the peninsula is an unspoiled and tranquil place with a flat shoreline and small seaside villages with prehistoric and mediaeval remains in their vicinity. There are frequent fish auctions at the quay in Portavogie, and below the 17th-century fortified farmhouse of Slane's Bay the 19th-century fishing vilage of Kearney has holiday cottages for hire. From Cloghy the main road turns inland to cross the peninsula to Portaferry where the motorist has the choice of crossing to Strangford by ferry or continuing up the eastern shore of the lough. This latter road goes by Kircubbin, where there is good sailing, to Greyabbey which has the well-preserved ruins of a Cistercian abbey founded towards the end of the 12th-century by a daugher of the king of the Isle of Man.

Newtownards; Movilla

At the head of the lough Newtownards, is a busy marketing centre with a Georgian town hall and a 17th-century octagonal Market Cross. Near the cross are the ruins of a 13th-century Dominican friary with a tower added about 300 years later, but by far the most important place in the district is Movilla where a famous monastery flourished in rigorous asceticism in the 6th century. The present ruins, however, are much later, later even than the hoard of Viking coins discovered at nearby Scrabo Hill where a cairn on the top was removed about a century ago to make way for the present tower.

Central Co. Down

Ballynahinch; Banbridge

From Newtownards a good road runs through Comber where there are important monastic remains from pre-Norman times, and down through the county to Ballynahinch — where another Michelin-starred restaurant is stylishly accommodated in the manor house of *Woodlands*. Another road wanders down along the fretted western shore of the lough, looking out towards the islands which provide an important bird sanctuary. To the west lies Dromore on the River Lagan, and further west and south is Banbridge which was the home town of Helen Waddell, author of the novel about Abelard and Héloïse. The River Bann flows through this pleasant little town, and in the main square, facing the Regency house where he was born, there is a monument to Francis Crozier, the explorer, whose persistence established the existence of the North-West passage between Canada and Greenland.

South of Banbridge lies Northern Ireland's 'Brontë Country' where the father of the famous novelists was born. The ruins of the Brontë cottage are about five miles from Loughbrickland — a village named for the poet, 'Bricriu of the bitter tongue' — and it was from this neighbourhood that the uncle or great-uncle on whom the character of Heathcliff was based set out to defend his niece's book from criticism — with violence if need be.

Strangford Loch

Killyleagh to Downpatrick

The little road by the shores of Strangford Lough goes through Killyleagh with its fine harbour and romantic castle to arrive at Downpatrick. The town is closely associated with Ireland's Apostle who landed about two miles away at Saul on his return to Ireland to convert the native population. The local chieftain, Dichu, was then living in a large Celtic rath which is now on the edge of the present town; he was duly converted and gave St Patrick permission to build his first church on the site now occupied by the cathedral. In the 12th century the Norman, John de Courcy, arrived and claimed to have discovered the grave not only of St Patrick, but of St Brigid and St Columba as well. All three graves are the subject of rival claims in other places, but since the 19th century St Patrick's alleged resting-place at Downpatrick has been marked by a large boulder — as if to settle the matter once and for all.

Although it incorporates parts of earlier churches, the present building of Down Cathedral dates mostly from the 19th century. Elsewhere in the town there is an 18th-century church with an earlier tower, and there is some fine Georgian architecture in the Mall. On the banks of the River Quoile outside the town there are remains of a 12th-century Cistercian abbey with three Early English lancet windows. On the summit of Slieve Patrick there is a shrine to the saint, while St Patrick's Wells are still thought to have miraculous healing powers.

A wealth of imagination is demonstrated in the conversion of part of the old County Down prison complex for museum purposes. The gatehouse and the former gaoler's house now accommodate the St Patrick's Heritage Centre and an impressive hoard of archaeological finds made on Cathedral Hill during the past five years. The oldest of these is a neolithic stone axe, but most of the discoveries date from the later part of the Early Christian era and include jewellery, pottery and a stone gaming board. Plans are now under way for the restoration of the three-storey cell block behind the gaoler's house.

Strangford; Ardglass
Hoards of ancient Celtic jewellery now in the Ulster Museum show this area to have been inhabited long before St Patrick's time, and it continued to attract settlers long after his death. There are mediaeval remains at Strangford, which is built on three levels above the double cove forming its harbour, and at Ardglass no less than seven small castles dating from the 15th-century onwards. There is a lifesize 14th-century stone statue of the Virgin and Child at Chapeltown, and at St John's Point, south of Killock, the ruins of a 10th-century church and a small, corbelled building.

South Co. Down
Mountains of Mourne
St Patrick apart, however, the Mountains of Mourne remain the chief pride of Country Down. This glorious range, which occupies the whole of the county south of Newry and Newcastle, is formed of granite, varying in colour from grey to pink and encircled and intersected by just enough roads to allow the motorist to explore them fairly thoroughly while still leaving vast tracts of untramelled landscape for walkers and climbers. The coast road from the seaside resort of Newcastle goes south beneath the highest peak, Slieve Donard, to the fishing village of Annalong, then on to Kilkeel which, with its 14th-century church standing in a rath in the middle of the town, is often called the 'capital of the Kingdom of Mourne'. A road leads into the mountain to 'Silent Valley' where vast lake reservoirs supply Belfast and its suroundings with water; the area is surrounded by a massive drystone wall and entrance is restricted to those holding permits issued by the Department of the Environment in Belfast.

Kilkeel to Newry
From Kilkeel minor roads run out to the fine beach of Cranfield Point, and to Greencastle where there is a splendid example of Norman military architecture of the 13th-century; but the main road runs above these and crosses the peninsula to reach Killowen on the northern shore of Carlingford Lough. At Rostrevor beneath a mountain forest mimosa and palm trees thrive in the open, while at Warrenpoint a 16th-century castle guards the lough waters which are still crossed freely by excursion boats going to and from the Republic. The Newry river estuary enters the lough at this point, and at its head stands the historic town built to defend the Gap of the North. It is said that

St Patrick planted the yew tree which gave Newry its name, and for centuries it has been a strategic centre between Slieve Gullion in Ulster and the Carlingford Mountains to the south in Leinster. The Newry Canal which runs through the town was the first commercial waterway of its kind in the British Isles, and the nice old 18th-century warehouses which line its quays are now used as stores.

Rathfriland to Bloody Bridge
Between Rathfriland, which stands on a hill north of Newry, and Newcastle on the coast, the village of Hilltown provides central access to the mountains. The road goes up through Clonduff Old Church and Bush Town, where there is a 'fairy' thorn tree, then turns right for Rostrevor, left for Slievenaman, or straight on for the reservoir with its magnificent views of the High and Central Mournes. There is a choice of walking tracks near the road junction above the Spelga Dam, while other paths lead into the 'Brandy Pad' and through the mountains by the 'Diamond Rocks' and the 'Castles of Commedagh' to come down again to the sea coast at Bloody Bridge.

County Armagh

Armagh City

The primacy of Ireland is vested at Armagh, and there are two cathedrals, both named for St Patrick. Like Rome, the city is built on hills and is one of the most handsome in Ireland with the finest concentration of Georgian architecture outside Dublin. Both cities, in fact, owe a great deal of their Georgian building to the Armagh architect, Francis Johnston.

Armagh was a place of importance long before Christianity. It was called *Ard Macha* after the warrior Queen Macha who ruled about 300 BC, and, outside the present city, built the great mound and earthworks known as *Eamhain Macha*. This was the seat of the Ulster kings for some six centuries, and in the last 300 years before Christ formed the headquarters of the Red Branch Knights; Cuchulain who was born, it is said of the *Dé Danann* god, Lugh, and a mortal called Dectera, was trained at *Eamhain* and went on to become the greatest of all Ulster's champions. As ever, there is some confusion about the names and dates of these legendary people, but it seems to be generally accepted that a chieftain called Daire was in control when St Patrick arrived, speedily converted him and received land for the establishment of church and monastic school.

Book of Armagh; Brian Boru
The 'Book of Armagh', which describes St Patrick's life, dates from early in the 9th century and is one of the finest illuminated manuscripts in existence. Unlike the cathedral which was destroyed and rebuilt

several times between the 9th and 11th centuries, it escaped the ravages of the Vikings, only to be pawned for £5 in the 17th century and remain lost for some 200 years. Its discovery during the 19th century brought it eventually to Trinity College, Dublin, where it may be seen in the Library today.

In 1004 Brian Boru visited Armagh and presented twenty ounces of gold to the church. Ten years later, after his death on the battlefield of Clontarf, he was brought to lie in state for twelve days in the cathedral, and a plaque in the present building marks the supposed position of his grave.

Cathedrals and Chief Buildings
Occupying the traditional site of St Patrick's foundation, the Church of Ireland Cathedral incorporates many fragments from earlier churches but is mainly a 19th-century restoration. The Roman Catholic Cathedral, which is situated on another hilltop approached by stepped terraces, is also a 19th-century building and has a great deal of elaborate marble work in its interior.

The wealthy and long-lived Archbishop Robinson, whose lifetime almost spanned the 18th century, was responsible for most of the fine building that distinguishes Armagh today. The old archiepiscopal palace, the public library, the Royal School, College Hill and the Observatory were all built under his patronage, and with his encouragement Francis Johnston went on to design the classical courthouse and the houses of the Mall.

North East Armagh

Garden of Ireland
Between the city of Armagh and the southern shore of Lough Neagh is a rich fruit-growing area which is often described as the 'garden of Ireland'. It is watered by the Blackwater in the west and the Bann in the east, and at its heart stands the tiny village of Loughgall where the Orange Order was founded in 1795. The occasion is commemorated by a small museum housing Orange sashes and documents and flags, while in the middle of the village a happy flourish of the rococo marks the entrance to Loughgall Manor demesne.

A pleasant network of leisurely driving roads stretches out from Loughgall, forming a circular route by way of elegant Ardress House and the Diamond, or going west to the villages of Charlemont, Blackwatertown and Tynan on the Blackwater river. On any of these quiet roads, on any quiet evening, it is common to see local men and boys lofting heavy iron balls along the way before them. The game, which seems to survive only here and in Cork is known as 'throwing the bullet' and the man who covers the longest distance in the least number of throws is the winner.

Ulster

Lurgan
Lurgan and Portadown are the most important towns in the north of Armagh. Both developed as centres of the linen trade, although supporting other industries at the same time, and are now growing gradually towards one another to form the 'lineal' city of Craigavon. Lurgan is a Plantation town established by William Brownlow in the 17th century, and it was a later member of this family who owned the near-invincible racing greyhound, Master MacGrath; there is a monument to the beastly paragon in front of Brownlow House, and another near Dungarven in County Waterford, where the name MacGrath is indigenous.

Portadown
Spanning the River Bann, Portadown forms a busy junction for railway lines to Dublin, Belfast, Armagh and Derry. A straight motoring road leads north-west out of the town to Lough Neagh, passing through the fenland district where the father of the American Civil War general, 'Stonewall' Jackson, was born, on its way. Another American association is New York's Coney Island, said to be named after the little off-shore Lough Neagh islet which may be visited by boat from Maghery near here.

South Armagh

The Fews; Slieve Gullia
Immediately south of Armagh the 'Fews' district comprises hills and woods of a gentle character quaintly at odds with the sinister overtones of Deadman's Hill near Newtownhamilton; this place was supposedly named for a highwayman of the notorious O'Hanlon family. Further south in the vicinity of Keady and Crossmaglen there are numerous antiquities, of which the most important is the 'Dorsey' pre-Christian defence. But the most conspicuous natural feature of the southern landscape of the county is Slieve Gullion, near the border with County Down. Surrounded by a chain of rugged hills, the 'whale-backed' mountain has a Bronze Age passage grave on the summit, while in the valley below a Stone Age dolmen stands by the roadside at Ballykeel. The region is vivid with folklore and legends, which may be investigated in the little local museum at Mullaghbawn.

Camlough to Temdragee
North of Slieve Guillion are Camlough lake, mountain and village, and then the granite model mill village of Bessbrook. There are six pubs in Camlough and none in Bessbrook, and between the two stands Derrymore House which is a splendid example of a thatched manor of the 18th century. Most roads around here converge on Newry in the neighbouring county, but the main northern route quickly re-crosses the boundary to travel along the old canal by Jerrettspass and Poyntz Pass to Tandragee on the Cusher river. There is a well-restored Georgian terrace in Tandragee, and the steep main street

climbs up to the entrance of an extravagant 19th-century Gothic castle — which makes its way in the modern world as a potato-crisp factory.

County Tyrone

Dungannon
This inland county with its fine mountain scenery, its glens and moors and river valleys, was the patrimony of that O'Neill family which held out against English invasion for so many centuries. Until the 17th century the principal O'Neill seat was at Dungannon, a steep, hilly town in the east of the county, but today only a mound on which their castle stood recalls the vanished earls, and the modern town is principally occupied with the manufacture of linen and cut glass. One of the most interesting buildings in it is the police station which is housed in a rather fancy 19th-century castle. This, it is alleged, happened when clerical confusion resulted in a fortress intended for the Khyber Pass being built in Dungannon instead.

South Tyrone

Castlecaulfield
A memorial to the great Hugh O'Neill stands in an old graveyard near a carved High Cross of the 9th or 10th century in the nearby village of Donaghmore, and here the Reverend George Walker was rector before he came to fame as the defender of Londonderry during the siege of 1689. His remains rest at Castlecaulfield about five miles away; and here more than a century later the curate, Charles Wolfe, wrote 'The Burial of Sir John Moore', an ode that was to excite the admiration of Byron and find its way into nearly every classical anthology of poetry. The church at Castlecaulfield is of 17th-century origin and has a sun-dial dating from 1685.

Benburb
South-east of Dungannon the villages of Moy and Charlemont face each other across the Blackwater river, and further on, where the river winds its way through a gorge, stands Benburb. The 17th-century castle ruins in the grounds of the Servite Priory occupy the site of an earlier O'Neill fortress, for this was an important outpost of the Tyrone defences and the scene of a major O'Neill victory in 1646; the parish church, which dates originally from 1618, contains a memorial to an officer killed in the battle.

Caledon to Clogher; Ballygawley
At Caledon to the south is the fine Georgian mansion which was the birthplace of Field-Marshal Alexander of Tunis, and to the west the fertile, wooded valley of Clogher reaches out along the border with County Monaghan: the quiet villages of Augher and Clogher and Aughnacloy make good bases for exploring the antiquities of the

region with plenty of forest and lake scenery to make the going attractive. One of the earliest stone crosses in Northern Ireland is at Errigal Keerogue, and at Knockmany and Sess Kilgreen there are carved passage graves. There is an old Tudor-style almshouse in Aughnacloy, and near Ballygawley the small farmhouse which was the home of the mother of the American president, Ulysses Simpson Grant. There are prehistoric remains in the countryside around Clogher, and in the porch of its small cathedral stands the *clogh-óir* or 'gold stone' believed to be an ancient pagan idol once covered with gold.

North Tyrone

Coalisland to Cookstown; Ardboe

One of the roads north from Dungannon goes through Coalisland which was the headquarters of a coal-rush in the 19th century: canals were built to the sea and dry wherries were constructed, but the venture was not successful and the old warehouses beside the derelict canal basin are now used as stores. An alternative northern route passes near Tullahogue, where the O'Neill chieftains were inaugurated, and goes by immense Killymoon Castle on its way to Cookstown. Drum Manor Forest Park, which has a garden devoted to the cultivation of butterflies, is near here, and in the vicinity of Dunnamore and Killucan there are stone circles, a court cairn and a dolmen. Away to the east on the shore of Lough Neagh is the magnificent Ardboe, nearly twenty feet high and elaborately carved; still more ancient tradition is represented at Ardboe by the annual Lammas Fair which attracts fiddlers and folk musicians from all over County Tyrone.

Sperrin Mountains

Half-way between Dungannon and Omagh, Pomeroy is the highest village in Tyrone and is considered a good starting-place for investigation of the antiquities of the Sperrin mountains. Further west Omagh, which is the chief town of the county, is situated in a wide valley at the foot of the south Sperrins. A good round trip from here is north through the Gortin Gap, on to the mountain village of Plumbridge in the Central Sperrins and back by Barnes Gap; a shorter excursion may be made by turning right through the Owenreagh valley to Sheskinshule and Creggan, then back down through Mountfield.

Camp Hill Folk Park

The main road north to Newtownstewart, however, goes by Camp Hill where a large folk park illustrating life in both America and Ulster in the 17th and 18th centuries is now complete. It is the result of funds donated by the American Mellon family, whose forebears came from the area, and the buildings include a duplicate of the original Mellon log house in Pennsylvania. At Newtownstewart the Duke of Abercorn's fine Georgian manor stands in the demesne of Baronscourt

Forest, while a mile outside the town stand the ruins of Henry Avery's Castle — allegedly the scene of nineteen successive executions of men who refused to marry an exceptionally ugly lady of the O'Neill family.

Strabane; Dergalt
There is a road west to the pretty villages of Castlederg and Killeter in the hills near the Donegal border, but the main road continues northwards through the model village of Sion Mills to Strabane. This agreeable agricultural town is situated on the River Mourne, where it joins the Finn to form Lough Foyle, and was the birthplace of the brilliant and prolific writer, Brian O'Nolan; his surrealist novel, *At Swim Two Birds*, was published under the pen-name, Flann O'Brien, and is considered a classic of Irish literature. In general, however, Strabane's ties with the United States are closer than those with Ireland, and amongst the emigrants from the town who became famous in America were John Dunlap, the founder of the first daily newspaper in the States, Alexander Orr who became president of the New York State Chamber of Commerce, and William Kerr who founded the Central Bank of Alabama. And from Dergalt five miles away went James Wilson, who became judge, newspaper editor and grandfather of President Woodrow Wilson; the farm were he lived as a boy is still in the hands of the Wilson family.

County Derry

Derry has an attractive, hilly landscape with fine beaches along the Atlantic in the north, and the Sperrin mountains forming the county boundary in the south. County Donegal in the Irish Republic is to the west, and in the east the River Bann marks the boundary with County Antrim.

Southern Co. Derry

Magherafelt
The little village of Ballyronan is Derry's harbour on Lough Neagh. A lakeside castle to the south was intended as the focal point of a town that never developed, although the London Salters' Company did go on to create a prosperous market centre inland at Magherafelt: wide streets radiate from its main square and there is a picturesque 18th-century court-house and gaol now used as a private residence.

Moneymore; Upperlands
Further south Moneymore has a wide Georgian main street. It has changed very little since the Drapers' Company built it, and an old-world atmosphere prevails around the market yard which is entered through an archway and has old corn stores with balconies.

Ulster

About a mile and a half from the town the National Trust maintains the 17th/18th-century architecture of Springhill House; its Dutch outbuildings contain a cottar's kitchen and a costume museum, while the main house has a fine collection of books, portraits and curios. A few miles away at Upperlands 18th-century linen mills still flourish under the direction of the family that founded them, while older history is represented at Dunglady by an earthen ringfort.

Bellaghy; Ballyscullion
Higher up at Ballaghy there is a good example of a fortified Plantation farmhouse with a circular tower and protective walls, and at Bally-scullion the scant remains of a palace built by the celebrated Bishop Hervey in the 18th century: the ruins look out across Lough Beg to a tower his lordship built on Church Island to improve the view.

Maghera
The Carntogher mountains rise in the north-west, and at the foot of the Glenshane Pass hill people and plainsmen meet and mingle in Maghera. Narrow streets and lack of formal planning indicate that this was a pre-Plantation town, and there are the remains of an 11th-century church with an impressive carved lintel hewn from a single stone.

Draperstown; Tobermore
The work of the London guild is also represented by Draperstown, where the mountains are scored by deep river valleys. At Poulmore the White Water forces its way through a deep, narrow canyon, and on its way to Lough Neagh the Moyala river runs through the pretty little single-street village of Tobermore, where St Columba is said to have learned his alphabet, and through Castledawson which has a fine, stone bridge.

Roe Valley
There is splendid scenery on the way to Glenshane Pass, and from there a route leads down into the Roe Valley and the meeting of three rivers at Dungiven; there is a prehistoric grave at Boviel, and further down, at Cashel, two old stone forts and the remains of an 18th-century mill said to have been held together by mortar mixed with animal blood.

Dungiven
Up to the 17th century Dungiven was a stronghold of the O'Cahan chieftains, and just outside the town in the ruins of an 11th-century Augustinian priory there is the sculptured tomb of an O'Cahan who died in 1385. The last of the O'Cahan chiefs died in the Tower of London in 1617, and the Skinners' Company laid out the foundations of the present town. Some of their fortifications are still standing, and parts of the early structure are incorporated in the present Tudor-Gothic Dungiven Castle which is used as a public hall.

Banagher Old Church
South of the town, near the biggest forest in the county, stand the
remains of Banagher Old Church with a lintelled doorway, square-
headed on the outside and arched within. This is attributed to an
11th-century saint of the O'Heney family whose descendants are said
to bring luck by sprinkling sand from the saint's tomb over 'anything
from a racehorse to a solicitor'. The tomb is a perfect small building
with a pitched stone roof and a sculptured figure of the saint at the
doorway.

Feeny; Claudy
The main road to the west runs through the old-fashioned village of
Feeny, passing within a few miles of an ancient sweathouse at
Ballydonegan. Claudy at the head of the Faughan Valley is a good
base for exploring the prehistoric antiquities of the neighbourhood,
but the main road continues on through the valley, bending north-west
for Londonderry.

Londonderry

The city takes its name from *doire,* the Irish word for 'oak', and is
said to have evolved from a monastery founded in a grove of oaks
by St Columba in the 6th century. Its situation on Lough Foyle was
ideal for the development of trade, and a busy commercial town grew
up — to be raided time and again by the Vikings between the 9th
and 11th centuries. Strangely enough, Derry was not captured by the
Normans, and it was not until after the 'Flight of the Earls' that it
became an English stronghold.

Bishop's Gate
The great walls, which still form daunting fortifications, were
completed with their original four gates in 1618. Two of the later
gates are dominated by stone watch towers, but Bishop's Gate, which
was rebuilt in 1789 and now forms a triumphal arch, is the finest of
them all. Siege cannon are still mounted dramatically on the walls
of Derry; the fiercest of them, eighteen-pounder 'Roaring Meg', dates
from 1642, though there are earlier cannon, including one presented
to the city by Queen Elizabeth in the collection facing the Guildhall.

Siege of Derry
The great siege of Derry took place in 1689 when James II's army
surrounded the walls and placed a boom across Lough Foyle to
prevent relief by sea; of the 30,000 people in the city, about 7,000
died of starvation. At an early stage Governor Lundy, who had Jacobite
sympathies, suggested admitting the army, but the apprentice boys
of Derry seized the keys of the city and locked the gates. Governor
Lundy fled, and his place was taken by the Reverend George Walker,
the rector of Donaghmore in County Tyrone: to the cannon ball fired
at the cathedral with James's terms for armistice, another replied

with the message 'No Surrender'.

The siege began in December 1688 and it was not until the following July that three Williamite food ships at last broke through the barriers on the Foyle and relieved the city. James II and his army marched away, and after them went Governor Walker to die at the Battle of the Boyne a year later. It is all kept very much alive in local memory by a ceremonial closing of the city gates every year and the burning of Lundy in effigy.

City Walls; St. Columb's Cathedral

Despite its troubles in both the distant and all too recent past, Derry conveys a bracing atmosphere of liveliness and good humour. The best way to explore is to start on the walls and follow them as far as military presence permits. Their expanse, some thirty feet in places, is varied by bastions and stone watch towers while, down below, the main streets of the inner city radiate from a central diamond to the four original gates. The most historic church inside the walls is the Anglican cathedral of St. Columb, which dates from 1613. Its chapter house holds the 17th-century locks and keys to the walls as well as Lord Macauley's manuscript account of the siege.

Chief Buildings

The Irish Society House built in 1764, the Regency-style former archepiscopal palace and the neo-classical courthouse are all in good condition. There is a striking memorial to the liberal Earl Bishop of Derry, Frederick Hervey, in the form of the 'Long Tower' church he built for the Catholic community a few yards outside the city walls, but by far the most impressive building remains the vast neo-Gothic guildhall with its oak-furnished council chamber and its series of stained-glass windows illustrating notable events in the city's history. The Catholic cathedral of St. Eugene has a flamboyant granite spire and a distinguished peal of bells that is operated mechanically.

Magee College; Prehen House

Inevitably, however, the city has developed far beyond its walls. The university buildings of Magee College are in the northern suburbs, and overlooking Lough Foyle at the point where the Jacobite forces put up their barriers is 18th-century Boom Hall. At Culmore Point there is a reconstructed Plantation fort, while near the City of Derry Golf Club descendants of the Knox family still live in Georgian Prehen House where a notorious tragedy took place in 1760. A local gambler called John Macnaghten attempted to kidnap a Mary Ann Knox of the time and in the course of a scuffle accidentally shot her. He was sentenced to death for the crime, but the hangman's rope broke and the crowd which was eagerly attending the execution shouted for reprieve. The prisoner, however declared that he did not wish to be known as 'half-hanged Macnaghten', climbed back onto the scaffold and hanged himself.

The Coast
Ballykelly; Limavady
The road north from Londonderry runs along by the eastern shore of Lough Foyle to Ballykelly, where there are the towers of a 17th-century fortification, and then on to Limavady. It was at Limavady that Thackeray fell in love with a local girl called Peg and wrote a long poem to prove it, and at Limavady many years later that Jane Ross took down the melody of the 'Londonderry Air' from an itinerant fiddler. This was O'Cahan territory before the Plantation, and its name, which means 'Dog Leap', derives from the story that the chieftain's dog jumped the river to carry a message for help to the Dungiven branch of the family. Today there is a six-arched bridge, dating from 1700, across the River Roe, and the faithful O'Cahan dog is commemorated by a carving on the chancel arch of the parish church.

Broighter: Celtic Gold
At Broighter in the marshy land between Limavady and the Lough, a farmer made a sensational discovery of early Celtic gold towards the close of the last century. Worked in the European *La Tène* style of very early times, the gold includes collars, a necklace, a bowl and a tiny exquisite boat equipped with sixteen miniature oars. The treasure is now in the National Museum in Dublin, and there are replicas in Belfast's Ulster Museum.

Magilligan
The route north from Limavady divides beyond the town to go by the 'Murderhole Road' across the mountains to Coleraine; or back towards the coast to Magilligan, where the largest beach in Ireland stretches out for more than six miles. The sturdy Martello Tower at Magilligan Point was built during the Napoleonic wars, while at the eastern end of the great strand the little resort of Downhill recalls the splendid and profligate Bishop of Derry, fourth Earl of Bristol, philanthropist, connoisseur and palace-builder extraordinary.

Bishop Hervey
Frederick Augustus Hervey was born in 1730 and became Bishop of Derry in 1776. Having almost tripled the episcopal revenues, he proceeded to spend them lavishly on antiques and works of art, and at Downhill built a palace which he reckoned would rival Blenheim.

A keen supporter of Catholic Emancipation, he attended the Covention of Volunteers in 1783, driving through the streets of Dublin in an open carriage with a regiment of gorgeously-costumed soldiers in his train. This bid for the presidency of the Volunteer movement did not succeed, but the Earl Bishop was not one to let reverses unsettle him and he continued his magnificent progress about the Continent, where so many Hotel Bristols are named after him. From his journeys he brought back many fine paintings, and at home built another palace at Ballyscullion on the banks of Lough Neagh and yet another at his family estate in Suffolk, England. To provide local employment he also built a road across the plateau of Eagle Hill and Binevenagh, a scenic route which affords splendid views between Downhill and Ballyhanna Forest.

Mussenden Temple

The Bishop's Irish palaces are ruined and roofless today, and his great collections scattered; but one exquisite monument to his memory remains in the Mussenden Temple at Downhill. Inspired by the vestal temples at Tivoli and dedicated to his lordship's cousin, Mrs Frideswide Mussenden, it is a perfect little building which stands at the edge of a cliff looking out over the Atlantic.

Coleraine

The main road from Downhill goes through Castlerock on its way to Coleraine. This important market and manufacturing town is situated on the banks of the Bann and has a new university which specialises in environmental and social sciences. There is a great deal of history in the area: at Ballintrees a hoard of Roman treasure, believed to be the result of Irish raids in Britain, was discovered during the 19th century; near the ruined fort of Mountsandel mesolithic flint implements were found.

There is excellent salmon fishing in the countryside outside Coleraine, and anglers will find accommodation to match in a spacious Georgian farmstead called *Camus House*. Macduff's Michelin-starred restaurant is within reasonable driving distance.

South of Coleraine

The fine seaside resort of Portstewart lies north of Coleraine, and to the south Garvagh makes a good base for exploring the country inland. Established early in the 17th century by the Canning family, which later gave England a prime minister, the village is situated on the Agivey river with a handsome forest beside it. There are cairns and a dolmen at Moneydig and Ballydullaghan, and at Ballintemple a schoolhouse stands inside an ancient rath. At Cuilbane there is a circle of pillarstones, and also the Slaghtavery cairn: this is said to be the grave of a dwarf called Averty who enchanted local women with his music, was killed by Fionn MacCumhail and buried head downwards.

County Donegal

Donegal is the northernmost county of the Irish Republic and shares the Northern Ireland border with Derry and Fermanagh; the border, in fact passes right through the town of Pettigo, leaving one half in Northern Ireland and the other in the Republic.

It is important to check approved routes with local authorities before driving from one part of the country to the other.

Southern Coastline

Along the southern approaches to Donegal the coastal vegetation begins to lean inwards away from the great gales blowing from the Atlantic, and thatched roofs are secured by ropes weighted with stones or tethered to pegs in the walls of cottages. The coastline is heavily indented and fragmented into islands, while inland magnificent scenery is formed by mountains, glens and lakes. It is a remote and lovely area, well worth the trouble of getting there, and peopled by clear-skinned men and women with extraordinarily bright blue eyes.

Bundoran; Ballyshannon
The bays and headlands shelter fine, sandy beaches, and the first of these is at Bundoran in the south of the county. A popular holiday resort with a good golf course, it lies between cliff ranges carved into strange shapes by the sea and named accordingly by local story-tellers. To the north the town of Ballyshannon rises on the steep banks of the River Erne, with Assaroe Falls nearby and the ruins of an ancient abbey, where an old water mill has been restored to working order. Near the abbey is a cave said to have been used by Roman Catholics during Penal times: it has a rough stone altar and two hollows believed to have served as baptismal and holy water fonts.

Lough Derg
Another of these 'Mass shelters', or *bothógs,* may be seen further inland near Pettigo, from which a road leads north to lonely Lough Derg. Surrounded by heathery hills and moorland, this is a place of pilgrimage in honour of St Patrick. Its half-dozen Early Christian stone oratories are known as the 'penitential beds', but most of the ecclesiastical buildings on the lake's tiny island are comparatively modern. Pilgrimages to the huge neo-Romanesque church built in 1921 still take place every summer.

Ballintra
Back on the coast the strange rock formations go on to Rossnowlagh, which has another fine strand. At Ballintra, further north, the Blackwater river flows through a series of caves known as the 'Pullans', then forms a waterfall by Aghadullagh Old Mill outside the village and flows on through a sixty-foot chasm. In the neighbourhood there are two megalithic tombs and a vast earthen fort associated with a High King of the 6th century.

Donegal Town

Donegal Castle
Donegal town is situated at the head of Donegal Bay where the main

roads from Derry and Sligo converge. Up to the beginning of the 17th century it was the principal seat of the O'Donnell clan, and the remains of a massive castle still overlook the River Eask from a rocky outcrop in the middle of the town. The original tower dates from mediaeval times, and beside it a later owner built a handsome three-storey gabled manor with a Jacobean door on the first floor.

Franciscan Monastery
Down on the seashore are the remains of one of the most important monastaries in Ireland. A 15th-century foundation established by the O'Donnells for Franciscan friars, it suffered badly in the inevitable conflicts of the next hundred years and was finally destroyed by fire resulting from the explosion of a powder magazine in a struggle between warring branches of the O'Donnell family. Today only the arcade of the cloister, the chancel and a gable of the south transept remain, but the ruins are still revered as the home of the Four Masters.

Four Masters' Gaelic History
These were four monks who undertook to compile the history of the Gaelic order in Ireland from its beginnings some 4,500 years before to its apparent end with the 'Flight of the Earls'. After their expulsion from the monastery around 1600 the Masters wandered from place to place, still working on their great annals which were completed in the 1630s. An original autograph copy of this valuable source of Irish history is in the library of the Royal Irish Academy in Dublin.

Lough Eask
About five miles inland Donegal's river broadens out to form Lough Eask, a tranquil lake with a wooded shoreline and the horseshoe-shaped range of the Blue Stack Mountains behind.

The Atlantic Peninsula

Mountcharles to Killybegs; Kilcar
The main road west, however, runs out along a stubborn Atlantic peninusula where the scenery grows wilder with every mile. It is tame enough at first, but above Mountcharles the glens and mountains assert themselves, moving down towards the coast behind Inver and Dunkineely to form massive ramparts beyond Killybegs. This land-locked little harbour is at its liveliest when the fishing fleet is in, but it has a wider claim to fame in the superb Donegal carpets which are woven there. The Donegal tweed industry has a centre about eight miles away at Kilcar, and traditional knitting and embroidery are carried on in cottages all over the district.

Slieve League; Malinmore
There are magnificent cliff scenery, caves and beaches along the coast west from here, and the village of Carrick is recommended as the starting point for the ascent of Slieve League. Although the summit is

less than 2,000 feet, this is not an easy climb and involves negotiating a precarious path along a cliff ledge with a precipitous drop of 1,800 feet to the sea on one side, and on the other a formidable escarpment rolling down to a forlorn lake. The road beneath continues out through Malinmore where there are a number of prehistoric tombs including a horned cairn and, off-shore, a tiny island with Early Christian remains.

Glencolumbkille
Tucked neatly between Glen Head and Malinmore, Glencolumbkille runs back from the water in a picturesque valley. There are two court cairns in the area, and a number of decorated stones, which may be early grave-slabs and now provide the occasion of a pilgrimage in St Columbkille's honour. Far more interesting, however, is the sociological phenomenon of Glencolumbkille's survival in modern terms. Here as in other poor parts of Ireland the emigration sparked off by the Famine continued into the 20th century, and it was the enterprising spirit of a local priest which reversed the trend by persuading the scant population to take an interest in co-operative farming, to start up cottage industries and a modern canning factory, and to create one of the best folk museums in the country,

St Columba's Birthplace
The valley is named for St Colmcille, better known outside Ireland as St Columba of Iona. Although he was born further north at Gartan — where there is a heritage centre in his honour — he is as popular as St Patrick throughout Donegal, and the people of this poor and lovely district are convinced that he founded a monastery here. Given the predeliction of the early Irish saints for inhospitable surroundings, they are probably right, and they can point to the site of a very early ecclesiastical foundation in support of their claim. This forms part of an annual pilgrimage to the Stations of the Cross on St Colmcille's Day, a ritual with a quaint element of paradox represented by several 'Stations' of pre-Christian origin.

Glengesh Pass
North of Glencolumbkille, beyond the Slievetooey mountains, lie the caves of Maghera, but the road turns back east into the mountains, winding through them to reach startling Glengesh Pass where it drops suddenly away, beneath the stern green face of the mountain opposite.

Lough Finn
Far below, the little town of Ardara is another good handcraft centre, and from there an inland road goes to Glenties, set in incongruously pretty, wooded scenery in the midst of rugged country; and then to Finntown and Lough Finn. This is the source of yet another Irish legend in which the hero, Fergoman, is attacked by a wild sow: the echoes of his cries for help rebounded from the cliffs opposite, misleading his sister, Finna, who plunged into the lake and swam to

and fro in pursuit of the echoes until she died.

The Western Coast
Inishkeel Island
The coast road from Ardara goes north to the villages of Narin and Portnoo on the southern shore of Gweebarra Bay. At low tide it is possible to walk out to Inishkeel Island where there are the remains of an ancient church. There are two ring forts at Dunmore Head, a large dolmen at Kilcloony and on an island in Lough Doon, a massive stone fort with a walk on the top of its walls.

The Rosses
The country further north is known as the Rosses — a wild landscape of scattered rocks and streams and tiny lakes becoming one with the Atlantic at Burtonport where the coast breaks up into dozens of islands. It is possible to go out to some of the islands by boat from the village of Bunbeg, and there is a regular ferry service to Aranmore.

Bloody Foreland
Just inland Gweedore lies tranquilly in the shadow of the glittering quartzite cone of Mount Errigal, but the coast road goes on to Bloody Foreland, so called for the colour of the rocky promontory at sunset; beyond lie the villages of Gortahork and Falcarragh looking out across Ballyness Bay to Tory Island.

Tory Island
Difficult of access because of rough seas which frequently prevent landing or departure, Tory still has a few hundred inhabitants, and its Early Christian remains — which include a Round Tower built of smooth beach pebbles — prove it to have been peopled for many centuries. Long before history, however, this was the home of Balor, one of the Fomorian pirates who drove the first settlers out of Ireland.

Giant Balor
A giant of thoroughly nasty propensity, Balor had only one eye; this was of appropriately cyclopean character, but all the same not sufficient to keep close watch on his daughter, Eithne, whom he incarcerated in a tower for safe keeping. Somehow a lover got in, or Eithne got out, and in due course she produced a family which the enraged Balor threw into the sea. All but one of the children turned into seals, and many years later the sole survivor, who was called Lugh and perhaps some relation of the *Dé Danann* god who fathered Cuchulainn, put out his grandfather's only eye and decapitated him for good measure. At Falcarragh a red-veined boulder is said to hold the blood of the father of Eithne's children — who was of course slain by Balor on the spot.

Life is hard in Tory where the land is barren and even the natural deposits of turf have been exhausted. Many families have emigrated to the mainland in recent years, but those who remain show remarkable resilience, making a living from the rich supplies of lobster and crayfish in the local fishing grounds and, wonder of wonders, subscribing to a vigorous school of painting. This remarkable phenomenon is attributed to the influence of the distinguished English painter, Derek Hill, who spends some time working on the island every year.

Horn Head; Doe Castle
From here on the mainland coast pushes out in a series of spectacular promontories, the first of them, Horn Head, rising 600 feet from the sea. By contrast the low ground at Dunfanaghy and Port-na-Blagh has fine beaches and holiday hotels, while from the village of Cresslough there is a nice excursion to Doe Castle with its moat hewed from solid rock on the landward side. This stronghold was contested by the rival clans of O'Donnell and MacSweeney, as well as the English, for centuries, but despite much bludgeoning survived into the 19th century as a dwelling place.

Rosapenna; Sheep Haven Bay
To the north the sea has smashed the coastline into countless strange shapes and peninsulas, with the tranquillity of vast, sandy beaches offering piquant contrast to the wild grandeur of the headlands. At Rosapenna, where there is a good golf course and a popular holiday hotel, one of these same beaches made history in the 18th century by submerging the local manor house and all the surrounding farms. Later there was a similar incident on the other side of Sheep Haven Bay when a landowner cut the holding grass from the sand, and older people still remember the contents of his submerged house being auctioned from the roof.

Rosguill Peninsula
At Downings, a few miles from Rosapenna, McNutts is worth a visit for anyone with an interest in fine Irish tweeds, and from here the circuit of the Rosguill Peninsula continues along a dramatic route known as the 'Atlantic Drive'. There are breathtaking views in all directions before the road descends to Milford, which is the starting point for yet another spectacular drive taking in the Fanad peninsula.

Fanad Peninsula
All along the western shore of the peninsula the sea creates rock tunnels as long as 300 feet and sometimes twenty feet wide and thirty feet high. The 'Great Arch of Dooghbeg' is formed by a massive rock detached from the mainland at its base and affording enough waterspace to permit the passage of a small boat.

The eastern shore is bounded by Lough Swilly and relatively sheltered along its southern reaches. There is good fishing and bathing at Portsalon, and in the seaside village of Rathmullen an excellent restaurant called *The Water's Edge*. But the most attractive place in the vicinity is the Georgian village of Ramelton. Several 17th-century houses survive here as well as a ruined church from the same period, and the handsome three-storied houses facing the tree-lined river are the pride of the village.

Central Donegal

Letterkenny
Letterkenny at the head of Lough Swilly is the ecclesiastical centre of the county, and has a modern cathedral. Near here, at Kilmacrenan, the great, flat-topped Rock of Doon marks the former inaugural place of the O'Donnell chieftains. Apparently this ceremony involved much unsavoury to-do with a white mare or cow, embracing and eating of same, plus immersion in the water used to cook the beast. Details of the ritual differ in various accounts but are uniformly unpalatable — and firmly discounted by later historians.

Glenveagh National Park
Some of the countryside west of Letterkenny is distinguished by areas of lush, fertile landscape at variance with wilder and more rugged scenery typical of Donegal. Much of it lies in Glenveagh National Park where the handsome neo-Gothic castle is now open to the public and gives access to famous gardens illustrating Italian, French and formal English landscaping styles.

Lake Garten
In the same neighbourhood, on the wooded shores of Lake Gartan, stands the Glebe Gallery, an enchanting small Regency house which was for many years the home of the painter, Derek Hill, and still contains his art collection and furniture. It, too, is open to the public. On the other side of the lake there is evidence of much thoughtfulness in the heritage centre situated amongst the remains associated with St Colmcille's birthplace. An invaluable booklet by John Tunney provides an informative context — economic, social and religious, — for the life of the saint and his times.

Inishowen peninsula

Inishowen
Inishowen is the last and biggest of the Donegal peninsulas. Spreading out from a narrow neck of land between Lough Swilly and Lough Foyle, it has a broad northern coast which culminates in Malin Head. The sheltered seaside resort of Buncrana is the principal town on the western shore, and makes a good base for excursions to the megalithic tombs in the vicinity.

Grianan of Aileach
A few miles south of Buncrana is the great 'Grianan of Aileach'.

According to the Annals of the Four Masters, the *grianan* or fort was built about 1700 BC and much later became a seat of the O'Neill kings of Ulster. It is situated on a hilltop commanding views of the two loughs, and has thirteen-foot thick walls terraced on the inside and penetrated by long lintelled passages. The fort was demolished by an O'Brien king of Munster early in the 12th century and lay in ruins until its reconstruction about a hundred years ago.

Dunree Head to Ballyliffen
A more recent fort, housing an impressive military museum, guards the approach to Lough Swilly at Dunree Head, and then the coast road goes on through the Gap of Mamore to Clonmany. There is a massive dolmen a few miles from this sheltered little village and ancient kitchen middens in the sandhills of Ballyliffen.

Malin Head to Inishowen Head
The road curves round then to Carndonagh where a souterrain with three chambers is hewn out of rock. From here a spur road runs twelve miles out through Malin and Ballygowan to Malin Head which is the most northerly point in Ireland. Although not very high, it gives fine views of the striking rock formations along the coast. The cliffs towards Glangad Head are close on 800 feet high, but the road stays south of them and goes down through Culduff and to Moville on the western shore of Lough Foyle. To the north, between Moville and Inishowen Head, the substantial remains of Greencastle are still protected by stout walls, and at Cooley there is a ten-foot stone cross with a hole through the upper portion and also a drystone 'skull house' believed to be a tomb-shrine.

Boating on the River Shannon

The Shannon and the Lakelands

The Shannon rises from a deep hole called the 'Shannon Pot' on a mountain slope in County Cavan. It is a mere stream as it sets out on its 200-mile journey south, but quickly gathers strength along the way, flowing sometimes as tranquilly as a canal between low banks, at others swelling out into great lakes which have the character of inland seas and the temperament to go with it.

Its length and the vast expanses of the lakes ensure that the Shannon is never crowded — so that the giddy shrieks of water-ski enthusiasts at Hodson's Bay or Killaloe do not carry beyond the waters in their immediate vicinity, and a regatta held by a yacht club on Lough Ree or Lough Derg will be invisible to pleasure craft further out.

Birdlife
The Shannon is irresistible to bird-watchers, and in autumn provides

a living chart of the movement of migrants. Resident birds include grebes, cormorants, herons, swans, snipe, curlew and dozens of others, while in winter large flocks of northern geese and other game birds fly in to join them.

Wildflowers
The waters in which they shelter are largely untroubled by commercial traffic, and the banks and lake islands of the Shannon nurture an immense profusion of wildflowers, many of them hardly known elsewhere in Ireland or Britain. *Inula salicina*, common in Europe and central Russia, grows lavishly on the banks of Lough Derg between Portumna and Dromineer, and in various areas there are 'Water Germander', 'Three-angled Bullrush' and the 'Salzburg Bright-Eye' more frequently associated with the Alps. The botany of the Shannon has not yet been fully explored, but enough of it is documented to afford material for a major thesis, and an endless source of excitement for enthusiasts, both amateur and professional.

Legend of the Shannon
Inevitably, there is a legend about the origin of the Shannon — going back once again to the *Tuatha Dé Danann* and the daughter of their great sea king, Lír.

At that time Connla's well, which has long since vanished, teemed with salmon, and the fish fed on nuts from the hazel trees overhanging the water. The nuts had the property of wisdom, and the salmon which ate them were distinguished by brillaint crimson spots; whoever ate these salmon became wise in turn. Women were forbidden within the precincts of the well, but the king's daughter, Sinnan, who was already beautiful and accomplished, was determined to be as wise as the men of her father's court. She made her way stealthily towards the well, but as soon as she approached the edge, the water surged up and overwhelmed her: her drowned body was borne along by the current as the water poured out of the well for ever and rushed through the countryside to form what is now the River Shannon.

Shannon Area
The combined length of the Shannon and its tributaries is well over 1,000 miles, and their drainage covers about a fifth of Ireland. The watershed is composed of cavernous limestone traversed by underground streams which create several river systems. The surrounding counties form the Irish lakelands, one of them belonging to the province of Ulster; Monaghan and Cavan are in the Republic, while Fermanagh is the southernmost inland county of Northern Ireland.

Fermanagh

Enniskillen
There is almost as much lake as land in Fermanagh, for the centre of

the county is entirely occupied by the vast waters of Lough Erne. On an island dividing the upper lough from the lower stands Enniskillen, the county capital, once the home of the Maguire clans but these days more popularly associated with the Royal Inniskilling Fusiliers and the Inniskilling Dragoons whose regimental banners hang in the cathedral. The name of the town, however, derives from the pre-historic woman-warrior, Cathleen, wife of the giant, Balor, who treated his family so badly on Tory Island.

Towering above the water, the Old Watergate and Castle of Enniskillen house two museums, and a little way outside the town a new theatre and arts centre has been built where the river curves attractively to enter the upper lake. Enniskillen is the principal shopping centre for cruisers taking on supplies — though there are shops in most of the villages along the shores — and there are plenty of restaurants. *Franco's Pizzeria*, which has a much more extensive menu than its name suggests, is one of the most popular.

Road Routes from Enniskillen
Castle Coole, one of the most distinguished houses in Ireland, is only a few miles from Enniskillen, while in the western suburbs is Portora Royal School which numbered Oscar Wilde and later, Samuel Beckett, amongst its pupils. A network of roads radiates from the town out into the county — going west to the cave complex known as the 'Marble Arch', south and north-east to the towns of Lisnakea and Irvinestown. A circular road runs round Lower Lough Erne, reaching out to the china-making village of Belleek on the county border.

Cruising on Lough Erne
But the best way to explore this lovely expanse of water is by boat, and great care has been observed in the development of facilities. The cruiser hire companies have voluntarily limited the scale of their activities to ensure quiet and uncrowded waterways, and a useful little booklet published by the Erne Charterboat Association at 50p includes a list of lakeside hotels, restaurants and bars as well as essential technical information.

Boa Island
Lower Lough Erne has nearly a hundred islands, most of them close to the shore and one, called Boa, linked to the mainland by a bridge at each end. A pair of two-faced statues in an old cemetery on Boa is almost certainly of pagan origin, for the druidic cult survived Christianity for some time in this isolated area, and as late as the 18th-century the islanders, although by now Christian, were reluctant to cross to the mainland.

White Island; Davey's Island
There are putative pagan remains on White Island too in the shape

of eight strange statues propped up in a row near a ruined church: they were discovered in the church walls during repair work in 1928, and their provenance still provokes heated controversy. There is no doubt, however, about the origins of the extensive monastic remains on Devenish, while on Davey's Island the discovery of mediaeval coins from several European countries suggests that the ruined church was once a place of pilgrimage.

Upper Lough Erne
Quiet roads reach out to Upper Lough Erne, where the shoreline is endlessly fragmented into islands, and it requires careful navigation to make a way between them, even by water. Near the cruiser station at Bellanaleck there is a good restaurant in a thatched cottage — and from there boats thread their way through the maze of islands, some of which are still inhabited. There is farming on Galloon, which has two lakes of its own, and on Trannish, and in the 15th-century Belle Isle was the home of Cathal MacManus who compiled the *Annals of Ulster*. There is a copy of the book in Trinity College, Dublin, and another in the Bodleian Library at Oxford.

Ballyconnel Canal; Belturbet
At the south-east end of the Lough the Woodford river forms the border with the Republic, and also the first stretch of the Ballyconnel Canal. For a while during the 19th century this linked the Erne with the Shannon and inland waterway enthusiasts clamour for its restoration. In the meantime, however, navigation of Upper Lough Erne ends at Belturbet in County Cavan, and it is worth remembering to change sterling into Irish currency if any serious shopping is contemplated here, as the exchange rate is usually in favour of the former.

Cavan and Monaghan
Loughs Emy, Muckno, Major
The counties of Cavan and Monaghan take pride in the fertile lakes which attract thousands of eager anglers every year. Most of the lakes in Monaghan are in the south, but Lough Emy, which is a favoured haunt of swans and wild fowl, lies to the north of Monaghan town near the border with Armagh.

The largest lake in the county is Lough Muckno at Castleblaney, and from there a road runs towards the west, by Lough Major at Ballybay, and on to the Rockcorry chain which spreads out in hilly, wooded landscape. There are more lakes near Carrickmacross further south, and also a worthwhile buy in the famous and exquisite lace which the old town still produces.

Walking and Riding Country
Both Cavan and Monaghan are blessed with pleasant, undemanding touring country, good for walking and riding. There is an excellent

equestrian centre at Glaslough near the lakeside castle which is the home of the Leslie family, and ideal walking country in Rossmore Forest Park. The history of the region is well documented in the prize-winning museum in Monaghan town, which has an 18th-century pedimented market house, now the property of the local tourist authority.

River Sources

No part of this gently undulating countryside is far from water, be it river or lake, and both the Erne and the Shannon have their sources in County Cavan. The former rises in Lough Gowna to form the labyrinthine waters of Lough Oughter at Belturbet, while the Shannon first appears on the lower slopes of Mount Tiltinbane in the Cuilcagh hills to the north west.

The River, its Lakes and Landscapes

Lough Allen

The Shannon drops more than 300 feet in its short journey to Lough Allen, which is the first of its lakes. The remarkable qualities of light and attendant cloudscapes, which are a considerable compensation for the uncertainties of Irish weather, manifest themselves with particular clarity near water, and at Lough Allen a kaleidoscope of limpid, subtle colour unfolds for miles across water and hillside.

Dromahaire; Tullaghan

This is County Leitrim, and the circular lake road turns off at Drum-keeran to run north-west through the county, past the massive ruins of Creevelea friary at Dromahaire, and out to Leitrim's only village by the sea. Tullaghan is flanked by excellent salmon rivers, and has interesting historical remains, including a 10th-century cross that was recovered from the sea late in the 18th century.

Iron Mountains; Slieve Anieran

The best view of Lough Allen is generally reckoned to be from the Iron Mountains to the east, while on the other side of the lake the caves and pits of Slieve Anieran attract intrepid pot-holers — who are obviously more interested in what cannot be seen than in what can. There are sluicegates at the southern end of the lough, and the view deteriorates considerably when these are opened to release the water in exceptionally dry weather. This does not happen too often.

Carrick-on-Shannon to Boyle

From Lough Allen a canal leads to the deep water of the Shannon and the marina at Carrick-on-Shannon, which is the country town of Leitrim. Cruising starts here, upstream through the village of Leitrim to the bright little town of Drumshanbo at the foot of Lough Allen, or westwards into the Boyle Water and the lovely reaches of Lough Key. There are the ruins of an abbey founded by the White Canons on one of the wooded islands, while to the south the Curlew Hills rise steeply above the water. At their feet lie the ruins of the 12th-century abbey of Boyle. This great Cistercian foundation took sixty years to build, and shows the dramatic change from Romanesque to Gothic in its architecture. It is considered one of the finest church remains in Ireland, and is in a reasonable state of preservation.

Rathcrogan; Castlerea
This is part of Roscommon, a gentle inland county belonging, like Leitrim, to the province of Connacht and bounded all along its eastern side by the Shannon. A number of ruined monasteries and castles show it to have been a region of considerable importance in the past, and in the middle of the county, at Rathcrogan and Tulsk, there are prehistoric remains associated with ancient kings and warriors: with the cattle-rustling Queen Maeve, with queens of the *Tuatha Dé Danann* called Éire, Fodhla and Banba and, much more realistically, with the later ruling family of O'Connor, whose present home, Clonalis House near Castlerea, is open to the public. It has a fine library and some interesting pictures.

Lough Corry to Jamestown
South of Carrick-on-Shannon the river loops smoothly through quiet country, widens out to form Lough Corry, then narrows again to curve away eastwards to Jamestown.

It is possible to follow the river by boat to Drumsna, where there are attractive but distinctly non-navigable rapids, though the main navigation goes by the picturesque canal known as the 'Jamestown Cut' to a point on the river above a new system of lakes.

Lough Tap to Lough Bofin
There is a relatively narrow stretch below Lough Tap, and then the water spreads out to east and west to form Lough Boderg and Lough Bofin and the Lakes of Carrandoe. They are all connected by natural channels or canals, and, between Boderg and Bofin, Derrycarne estate pushes gently out into the water on a rounded promontory. The village of Dromod on the shore of Lough Bofin has a nice little harbour and gives access by road to other lakes in the east of County Leitrim.

Meeting of three Counties
Going on south by the river, the village of Rooskey spans the Shannon and marks the meeting of Counties Roscommon, Leitrim and Longford. Above the mooring at Rooskey a tiny shop-cum-enormous-bar is run by a genial proprietor who sends all over the county to fulfil his cruising customer's orders, and will as readily provide bunting to deck a boat for someone's birthday as a pound of onions for Irish Stew. The village makes a good base for excursions into Leinster and Connacht. To the east there is a splendid 17th-century castellated manor at Newtownforbes and further on, in Edgeworthstown, the

Georgian house in which the novelist, Maria Edgeworth had her home as a child.

Granard
In north County Longford the busy market town of Granard is the scene of an annual harp festival, an event which originated there in the eighteenth century and was revived within the past ten years. The town is a convenient base for anglers fishing the River Inny, or Lough Gowna and Lough Sheelin.

Lough Forbes
From Rooskey the Shannon goes on south to enter Lough Forbes, below which the villages of Cloondara and Termonbarry face each other across a weir and again provide good bases for exploring the hinterland to east and west. But the river continues on its quiet course to Lanesborough where it enters Lough Ree.

Lough Ree
This is one of the biggest lakes on it and should be approached with as much prudence as admiration. Sixteen miles long by six miles at its widest point, Lough Ree receives very little shelter from its flat shoreline and can be dangerously windy at times: before embarking on its waters, it is wise to consult local watermen and be guided by their advice no matter if it seems excessively cautious. This done, Lough Ree presents a fine stretch of sailing and cruising water with countless fascinating bays and inlets.

Hare Island
Hardly any of its islands are inhabited any more, but several of them have the remains of ancient monastic foundations, and in calm weather cattle are swum out to graze on Hare Island which has massive stone harbour walls.

Rindoon Point
At Warren Point there are the substantial remains of a heavily-fortified mediaeval town, and at Rindoon Point a 13th-century castle stands on a rocky peninsula looking out over the broadest part of the lake. It is said that the much-travelled Queen Maeve met her death in Lough Ree, and few will suggest that this was not long overdue.

Roscommon Town
The county town of Roscommon is within feasible striking distance from the west shore at the northern end of Lough Ree, and is worth a visit for the sake of its immense castle, in ruins now like so many others throughout the country but showing rare strength and dignity in its great round bastions and towers. The ruins of Roscommon Abbey are also impressive, while only five miles away at Fuerty history is for once reversed in the form of a German religious order living in a restored castle dating originally from the 12th century.

Athlone

History

Below Lough Ree the river enters Athlone, which is its principal town and the busiest crossing-point from the east to the west of Ireland. Situated almost at the exact centre of the country, it has been a ford since very early times and always a point of vital strategic interest: whoever commanded Athlone controlled the principal approach to Connacht, and inevitably it was a source of conflict between English and Irish, and before them between Irish and Irish.

As often as the O'Conors of Connacht built wattle bridges and fortified the western bank, the O'Melaghlin clans rampaged out of Leinster and destroyed them. But order was imposed, at least for a while, in 1001 when Brian Boru sailed his fleet up the Shannon and convened his armies at the ford.

With the arrival of the Normans the defences of Athlone were form-alised, and the walls were completed in 1257. Today the castle built earlier under the supervision of King John still dominates the bridge of Athlone and, although modified to meet the exigencies of later centuries, retains its original keep behind a forty-foot curtain wall. Some fragments of the original defensive town walls also remain, but the batteries on the western edge of the town date from 1798.

Athlone changed hands so often during various wars that it is a wonder the civilian population chose to stay there. Its proudest hours were during the Williamite siege of 1691 when a small force of some hundreds of Jacobites held off Ginkel's army for days, then rushed out in successive volunteer groups to hack down the bridge as the enemy advanced across it — all to no avail in the end for, although the bridge was destroyed, the respite was brief, and superior numbers and equipment forced the Irish back into Connacht for their last sad stand at the Battle of Aughrim.

Shannon Boat Rally

A more cheerful atmosphere animates Athlone today, and the town is at its liveliest towards the end of July when craft from all over Ireland converge for the Shannon Boat Rally. The purpose of this is not quite clear, but it is reported to be a very jolly affair, with com-petitions which so far have resulted in no fatal accidents — despite the competitors' propensity for falling overboard at an advanced stage of the proceedings. The Rally extends up as far as Carrick, and during the hectic week of its duration it is alleged that there are helmsmen on the Shannon who would benefit by lessons from New Year's Eve drivers.

There are plenty of hotels in Athlone, including one with a beautiful situation outside the town at Hodson's Bay which makes Athlone an excellent base for exploring central Ireland.

To the immediate west is County Galway, which is dealt with in Chapter III of this book, and to the east the two Leinster counties of Westmeath and Offaly, both of which deserve to be better known than they are.

County Westmeath

Moate to Tyrrellspass
Only a few miles out of Athlone on the Dublin road, in the thriving town of Moate, a tall, rectangular castle of the 16th century is still inhabited and its owners hold title deeds dating back to 1656. On the same road, at Kilbeggan, a disused distillery has been converted into a crafts centre with its old water wheel turning again, and at Tyrrellspass a 15th-century castle built by the family which gave the village its name is in use again as a private residence.

Oliver Goldsmith Country
Just north of Athlone, beyond the village of Glassan, is Lissoy which is perhaps more popularly known as 'Auburn' and the inspiration of 'The Deserted Village'. Goldsmith was born a few miles away at Pallas, and the ruins of his childhood home in the rectory of Lissoy may still be seen. The Goldsmith Country is well signposted for tourists, and includes a pub called 'The Three Jolly Pigeons', although all authorities are adamant that this had nothing to do with 'She Stoops to Conquer' — but if not, why not?

Hill of Uisneach
Near Ballymore in the same district the Hill of Uisneach is said to mark the point where the Firbolgs divided Ireland into four provinces. King Tuathal, of the *Dé Danann* tribe which ultimately drove the Firbolgs out of the country, arrived from Connacht and added an extra province comprising the present counties of Meath and Westmeath. He marked the spot with a vast boulder called the 'Catstone' and, although the fifth province has long since been re-absorbed into the original four, this thirty-ton rock still stands on the hill along with several other prehistoric monuments.

Loughs Ennell, Owel, Derravaragh
Westmeath is lakeland country, and the county town of Mullingar lies between the two largest which are Lough Ennell and Lough Owel. It was in the latter than King Malachy I drowned Turgesius the Dane who had desecrated Clonmacnoise, and the King himself ended his days on an island in the other lake. To the north lies Lough Derravaragh, where the Children of Lir wandered as swans for 300 of their 900 years' exile from humanity.

Tullynally to Lough Sheelin
At Tullynally the 19th-century Gothic mansion of the Pakenham family,

Earls of Longford, is open to the public. At Fore, near Lough Lene, important monastic remains include a 10th-century church with a baptismal font installed about two hundred years later, and also imposing priory ruins with square towers and loop-hole windows. Two gates survive from the late mediaeval town walls of Fore, and out on the Castlepollard road there is a tower named for an anchorite of the 17th century. North of this area three pretty lakes along the county border lead to the famous dappling waters of Lough Sheelin, which is shared by the counties of Westmeath and Cavan.

County Offaly

Bog of Allen
Although the Slieve Bloom mountains rise in heathery outline to the south-east, most of County Offaly is covered by the great Bog of Allen which constitutes Ireland's main source of native fuel. For botanists and archaeologists the bog has a special fascination of its own, revealing myriad plants and flowers to those with the patience to seek them out, preserving dug-out boats and prehistoric weapons for thousands of years beneath its soft, springy soil. For the motorist, however, bogland can become rather dull if it goes on very long, but there is plenty of contrast in County Offaly. A town called Daingean here was named Philipstown after Philip II of Spain until recent times, and there is a famous distillery not far away in the county capital of Tullamore.

Durrow; Birr
At Durrow only a High Cross and some scant ruins recall the famous abbey where the Book of Durrow was compiled c. 700 AD, but in Birr the charm of Georgian design remains intact.

After the usual stormy history, this townland came into the hands of the Parsons family and was laid out, much as it is today, on the spacious and elegant lines favoured by planners of the late 18th century. The Parsons in time became the Earls of Rosse, and the present Countess is Princess Margaret's mother-in-law. Their 19th-century Gothic castle at Birr has magnificent grounds which are open to the public, and in the park stand the walls and cylinder of the telescope developed by that distinguished astronomer, the third Earl of Rosse. The giant telescope, which weighs about four tons, is now in the Science Museum in London.

Clonmacnoise
The Shannon forms the western boundary of County Offaly, and on its banks below Athlone stand some of the most extensive monastic remains in Ireland. Clearly visible from the river, and accessible also by road, Clonmacnoise rises in peace and loneliness above green fields: it has a wonderful atmosphere of quiet dignity, its troubles all in the past, its future as a cherished monument secure. It was founded

Shannon and the Lakelands

by St Ciaran in the 6th century and endowed by various Irish kings in the following centuries; Turgesius the Dane did his best to bring it down, but it survived his ravages, and many other vicissitudes and remained active until the Reformation. The churches, castle, crosses, round tower and inscribed grave slabs occupy a considerable area and are worth a lengthy visit by anyone sensitive to strong auras of the past.

Shannonbridge

The river flows very quietly — respectfully almost — past Clonmacnoise and makes it way down to Shannonbridge where a fine sixteen-arch bridge marks the meeting of Offaly, Galway and Roscommon. A few miles south the Grand Canal from Dublin joins the river at Shannon Harbour.

Canal Diversion to River Barrow

At this point it is possible to branch off and cruise by Tullamore, Daingean and Edenderry to Robertstown where a spur of the canal turns south, passing Rathangan near the Hill of Allen and Monasterevan with its ancient drawbridge, to join the River Barrow at Athy. Before choosing this route however it is important to consult the cruiser hire company involved, as river craft are not always suitable for the canal, and vice versa.

The River Barrow flows through some of the loveliest and most civilised landscapes in the gentle province of Leinster. It is navigable down as far as St Mullins, and the prettiest scenery is in the lower area around Graiguenamanagh where the early 13th-century Cistercian abbey of Duiske has recently been restored for public worship. It is a tranquil part of the country, best suited to those of leisurely disposition with an eye for the less spectacular beauties of nature.

At the head of Lough Derg, Portumna, with its 17th-century castle and great Jacobean garden, is the site of the most recent marina on the Shannon. This is the headquarters of the Emerald Star fleet, and is a popular starting-point for cruise package holidays arriving at Shannon Airport.

Lough Derg to Limerick

Twenty-five miles long and averaging between two and three miles in width, Lough Derg is the largest of the Shannon lakes; most people also consider it by far the loveliest. Gentle hills rise behind its banks and the land becomes more fertile with every mile as the water moves south into the province of Munster.

Inis Cealtra Island

Along the banks are tiny villages like Scarriff and Mountshannon, friendly hospitable little places, well used to visits from passing cruisers and capable of coping with every emergency — including, at

170

least once, the sudden necessity of removing and confining a wayward crew member who had suddenly gone berserk. But the lake itself is even more charming than its surroundings and it is possible to visit some of its many islands, including Inis Cealtra which has mediaeval monastic remains.

Rapids
At the foot of Lough Derg, below the town of Killaloe, the Shannon leaps forward in a dramatic series of rapids and torrents. In the short passage south to Limerick it drops about a hundred feet, and at Ardnacrusha is harnessed to provide power for the huge turbines of the Shannon Hydo-Electric Scheme. A tail-race leads the water back to Limerick and beneath the city the tidal estuary widens out to form a major sea-way.

The hair-raising journey down to Limerick is fully navigable but calls for considerable experience and skill. Wisely, cruiser-hire companies do not permit their craft to go below Killaloe.

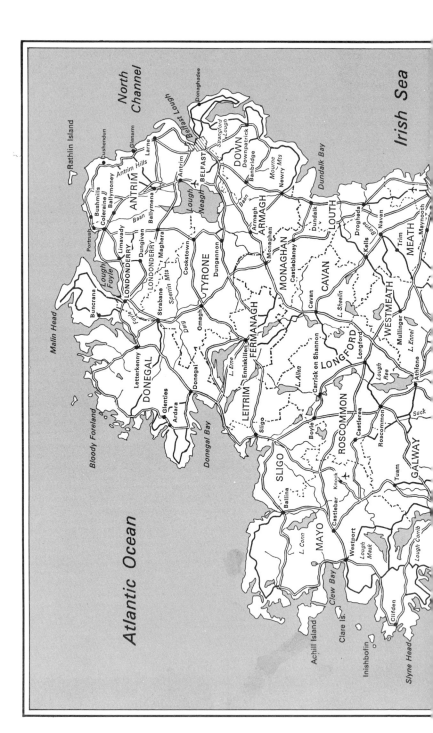

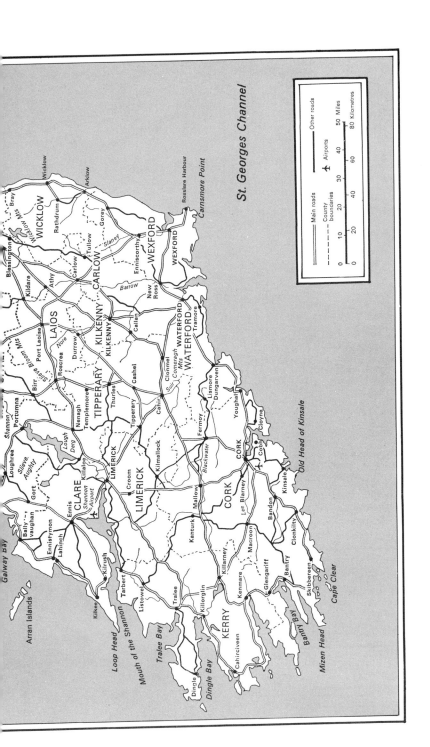

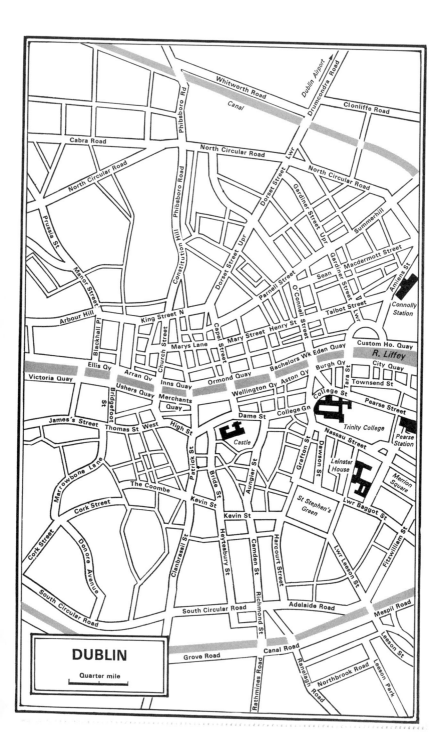

DUBLIN

Quarter mile

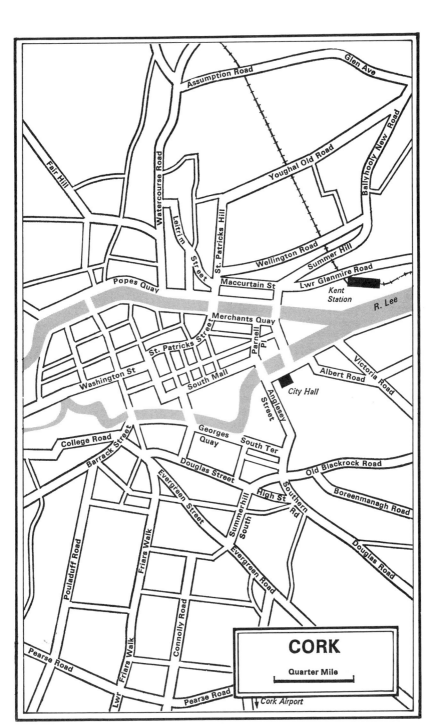

CORK

Quarter Mile

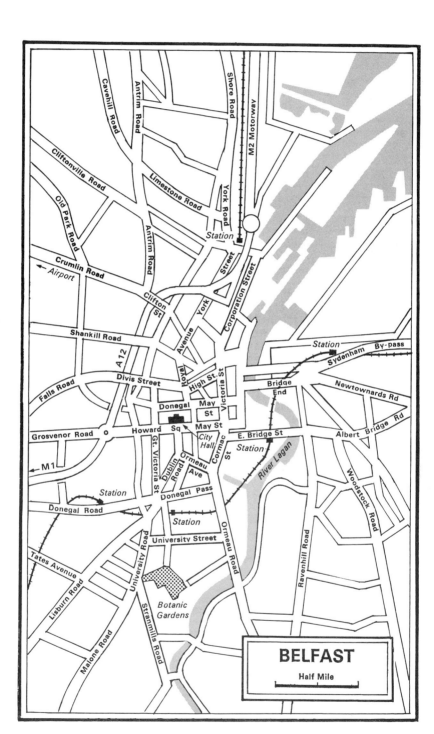

BELFAST

Half Mile

Index